MEN *and their* HORSES

THERAN PRESS

THERAN PRESS IS THE ACADEMIC IMPRINT OF SILVER GOAT MEDIA.

THERAN IS DEDICATED TO AUTHENTIC PARTNERSHIPS WITH OUR ACADEMIC ASSOCIATES, TO THE QUALITY DESIGN OF SCHOLARLY BOOKS, AND TO ELITE STANDARDS OF PEER REVIEW.

THERAN SEEKS TO FREE INTELLECTUALS FROM THE CONFINES OF TRADITIONAL PUBLISHING.

THERAN SCHOLARS ARE AUTHORITIES AND REVOLUTIONARIES IN THEIR RESPECTIVE FIELDS.

THERAN ENCOURAGES NEW MODELS FOR GENERATING AND DISTRIBUTING KNOWLEDGE.

FOR OUR CREATIVES, FOR OUR COMMUNITIES, FOR OUR WORLD.

WWW.THERANPRESS.ORG

 A portion of the annual proceeds from the sale of this book is donated to the Longspur Prairie Fund.
www.longspurprairie.org

Aristophanes
MEN *and their*
HORSES

Translation by
MIKE LIPPMAN *and* **WILFRED E. MAJOR**

Preface by **JEFFREY HENDERSON**
Introduction by **ROBERT HOLSCHUH SIMMONS**

THERAN PRESS

To John Oliver and every other modern Aristophanes.
Keep fighting the good fight while making us laugh!

CONTENTS

ACKNOWLEDGMENTS

Thanks for the spectacular feedback and patience from the Theran Press team, as well as from our anonymous readers.

Thanks also to all those who helped us and gave us feedback along the way as we worked from iteration to iteration. Special thanks to those who participated in the dead-cold test reading at CAM-WS 2020: Brooke Adam, Nichole Brady, Peter Burian, Krishni Burns, Stephen Cass, Ellie Churchill, Amy Cohen, Garrett Conte, Seth Jeppesen, Mary-Kay Gamel, Rob Groves, Craig Hardiman, Jeff Henderson, Ellen Kratzer, Vanessa Larsen, Laura Lippman, Matthew Loar, Ethan Ostdiek, and Amy Pistone.

PREFACE

Aristophanes' *Knights* is a landmark in the history of both theater and democracy: our second-oldest surviving comedy, produced for a national Athenian audience in the winter of 424 BCE; the first drama wholly devoted to an overt attack on a contemporary political leader; and the first portrayal of populism, a style of leadership to which Aristophanes applied the never-bettered term "demagogy." *Knights* is also a flat-out Aristophanic masterpiece, a first-prize winner at its debut and prized in antiquity among the master's canonical works for its vigor and wit, for the sheer force and exuberance of its poetry, and for the brilliance of its satire. And yet *Knights* is perhaps Aristophanes' least-known play in modern times, rarely translated and seldom performed, hardly ever assigned in college—forget about secondary—courses, and of scholarly interest mainly to the more intrepid among political scientists. But given the rise of populist nationalism in recent years both in the United States and abroad, it would seem that *Knights* is overdue for a serious revisitation.

Certainly, the Athenian situation as the play begins should strike a chord today. In the audience were members of the oldest and greatest living generation, who had repelled the Persian invasions, established the world's first democracy, and made Athens an unprecedentedly prosperous imperial power. But following the death in 429 BCE of Athens' long-time leader, the Olympian aristocrat Pericles, a series of populists from the commercial world—rather than the traditional landed elite—had suddenly captured the allegiance of the people, not least its greatest generation: as we hear in *Knights*, political leadership was no longer a job for "the well-educated. Nor for men who are decent and well behaved. It's for the ignorant who love to roll in the dirt." Out of nowhere, it seemed, there had arisen a series of demagogues, snake-oil salesmen from the lower-order trades, each worse than the last and therefore more powerful, ending most recently with a loudmouthed bully, Cleon. Now Athens was in the grip of fake news and conspiracy theories, divine oracles manufactured to bolster Cleon's power, the people divided into partisan camps, decent citizens rich and poor alike cowed into submission. Cleon, who was fond of comparing himself favorably with great leaders of the past, enjoyed browbeating the generals, taking credit for the accomplishments of others, norm-breaking and norm-bashing, sexual opportunism, branding the elite as traitors and harassing homosexuals—a category he associated with the elite—gulling the people with flattery while using his authority to line his own pockets, screaming, insulting, intimidating, slandering, shaking down the wealthy, oppressing Athens' allies, and always shamelessly lying. Athens was not becoming great again, as Cleon boasted, but merely a town of chumps. As we might ask today: What's the matter with Kansas? Aristophanes asked: What was to be done to save the Athenian people from their self-defeating allegiance to a scoundrel?

Knights offers a beguiling allegorical fantasy. Mr. Demos, a kind of Uncle Sam personifying the people, has turned senile, so that his prosperous household (Athens) has been taken over by a new-bought barbarian slave, Paphlagon, a tanner like Cleon, a liar, a flatterer, and a manipulator who has won the master's confidence and sidelined the loyal slaves by turning the master against them, all the while siphoning off all the household's goodies for himself. In despair, the loyal slaves steal Paphlagon's stash of oracles and discover his terrible secret: he is fated to be replaced by someone even lower than a tanner—a sausage seller! With the backing of the elite corps of Knights, who in actuality had their own reasons for hating Cleon, the slaves recruit such a sausage seller, convincing him that his low birth, marketplace morals, and near-illiteracy are the perfect ingredients for success. The sausage seller challenges Paphlagon to a series of contests in shameless demagogy, with Demos as judge.

Can this end well? What happens if someone even lower than Paphlagon does win the allegiance of Demos? Or is the sausage seller more of a worthy savior than initially meets the eye? What happens to Paphlagon if he loses the contest? In any scenario, will Demos ever come to his senses and be the kind of Demos that he used to be? The reader is invited to find out.

And so I am happy to introduce this new translation of a great political comedy that, once again, in the current chapter of our democratic experiment, could hardly be more relevant. It is a translation unafraid to capture the tone and force of the original and to cast its politics in contemporary terms—what's not to like about a Paphlagon called Drumpf?—without sacrificing accuracy and pace. All the play's jokes and thought-provoking satire come through without the need for footnotes, and as might be expected from a pair of experienced classical troupers and award-winning teachers, the translation is both eminently readable and performable.

So get out your popcorn and barf bag, fasten your seat belts, and have a look into the wonderful mirror that Aristophanes presents!

JEFFREY HENDERSON

TRANSLATORS' PREFACE

This translation began as a challenge, a response to the notion that this play was too specific to its original time of performance to be accessible in the 21st century. We both believed that the play was a specimen of perennially great theater, but it was unappreciated and rarely performed. Plus there were few English translations available, none beyond those that completed sets of Aristophanes translations, and none with the dynamics of live performance in mind. Ironically, *Knights* became painfully relevant, with the election of Donald Trump to the White House, since, in our eyes, he is eerily similar to Cleon, the comic target of this play. Just as Cleon in the play has no sense of humor and lashes out when attacked by comedians, so does Trump seem to be unable to take a joke. Thus, as Aristophanes barely conceals Cleon's character by using the pseudonym "Paphlagonian" (a slur that means literally something close to "Poofistani," but no one in the audience would be confused about whom he was targeting), we chose to name the character "Drumpf" (thank you, John Oliver!), thinking that it would be self-evident whom we were satirizing. In many specific references along the way and in the triumphant resolution, however, Aristophanes will surely remain fascinating and challenging. What he dramatizes as the way to make America—er, Athens—great again, will find elements of support and opposition in every caucus. We like to think conversations about why this is so would please Aristophanes, committed as he was to dialogue about the strengths and weaknesses in the democracy of his native community.

A point we wish to emphasize: this is a *translation*, not an adaptation. That blunt assertion may surprise the modern reader. We worked through the original Greek word for word, but converting the Greek into contemporary English meant modernizing concepts, not to adapt them, but to translate them. For example, we chose to morph Greek deities into the rhetorical point of their identification in context ("Athena" becomes "Lady Liberty" to translate the patriotic invocation of the goddess) and avoided esoteric jokes about individual Athenians and puns that did not hold up for a hundred years, much less 2,500. The sausage seller becomes a hot dog man and a Greek word that etymologically refers to "someone who will do anything" (in a negative way) becomes the modern politically charged "Deplorable," and so on, but always with the goal of transmitting the jokes and gut punches that Aristophanes delivered in 424 BCE. More often, statements that seem flagrantly modern are so because Cleon was a businessman of shady reputation who became a demagogue known for his aggressive speech and unfiltered attacks on the "intellectual" elites of Athens who would not side with his policies, a phenomenon repeated daily in the country as we were translating.

The line numbers printed in this text match up with the line numbers in the original ancient Greek; to reflect modern dramatic practice, some sentences may have been broken up into shorter bursts but were originally part of the same line.

It could seem as if our translation is a little dirty, perhaps not what might be expected from the reputedly sophisticated culture of ancient Athens. Trust us. We didn't do Aristophanes as much justice as he deserved. His Greek oozes with far more filth than we could pack into our translation.

Aristophanes' play was also a musical spectacle. The chorus of cavalry riders for whom the play is named sang and danced numerous times during performance. Of these performances, only the lyrics of the songs are left in the script, no music and no choreography. In order to fire the imagination of readers—and directors and performers (hint hint)—we have invoked a range of music and song. Although Aristophanes sometimes parodied other songs, we offer not direct parodies but have indicated a song with each choral section that served as inspiration, and in doing so we have tried to summon a range of styles and sources, much as the meter of Aristophanes' lyrics suggest that he invoked and mixed numerous musical performance traditions. Ideally, our lyrics will strike readers and audiences as humorous and outrageous.

In one section of the play, to be candid, we did take extra liberties: the *parabasis*. Here, in antiquity, the playwright (via the chorus) took liberty to address whatever topics he chose, not necessarily bound to the action of the rest of the play in any traditional sense. We decided, using Aristophanes as our muse, to translate in our own voices, addressing the difficulty of translating Aristophanes, and the larger problem of translation as scholarship. Much of what we say is, still, a translation, albeit with greater liberty—translations which preserve the specific topics of Aristophanes' parabasis are available elsewhere. We recommend the Loeb translation by our esteemed preface writer, Jeffrey Henderson. Aristophanes expressed concern that his comedy would not be taken seriously. We similarly are concerned that our academic exercise, which, while fun, might not be treated with as much respect by our peers. But translating, especially comedy, means merging comprehension not just of two languages but two cultural contexts widely separated in time and place. For us, this is, in its highest respect, a creative blending of both our research, our teaching, and our service (to you!).

We hope you enjoy it! Finally, in our humble opinion, if desperate laughter about demagoguery is even slightly less necessary as you read it than when we undertook this project, then thank fucking god.

MIKE LIPPMAN
WILFRED E. MAJOR

INTRODUCTION

Men and Their Horses, more commonly known as *Knights* in English, is a comic play composed by Aristophanes and first performed in Athens, Greece, in 424 BCE. It is among the few ancient Greek plays that have survived through the millennia, copied from manuscript to manuscript hundreds of times. Why did it make it through all of that time, when the vast majority did not? One answer, of course, is chance—many highly regarded works have been lost through uncontrollable circumstances. Another answer, though, is the long-recognized brilliance of this work, on many counts, among which are the following: 1) it is simply funny, with a humor that holds up nearly 2,500 years after its initial production; 2) it demonstrates the power of theater, in a free society, to express dissent against a public figure through dramatic mockery; 3) it portrays the intensity of a city involved in a years-long military conflict, and of efforts to offer praise or blame in the fog of war; 4) it is the only example of Athens' first demagogue, Cleon—albeit a greatly exaggerated version of him—engaging interpersonally with common Athenians; 5) it provides an example, though hyperbolic, of the Athenian institution of pederasty and of the gray lines between it and friendship. Elaboration on those matters, and more, will come in the pages to follow, and in the play itself.

ARISTOPHANES AND HIS PURPOSE IN *MEN AND THEIR HORSES*

The author and director of *Men and Their Horses*, Aristophanes (born as early as the 450s BCE and as late as 445, and died around 386 BCE), could have been as young as 21 when the play was produced, in 424 BCE. This was just his fourth public play—following *Banqueters* in 427, *Babylonians* in 426, and *Acharnians* in 425—and just the first of the plays he wrote that he directed himself.

Beyond the jitters of being a first-time director at a major theater festival in Athens (which was then an independent city-state, like the rest of the cities in what is now Greece), he had at least one other big reason to be nervous about this foray into Athens' annual theater competitions. In this play, as you will read, he directly attacks Cleon, the most powerful politician in Athens at the time. When he did the same in a much less direct way two years earlier, in *Babylonians*, Cleon sued him for slander; the outcome of that suit is unclear. And indeed, oblique references in *Wasps*, the comedy that Aristophanes produced in 422 BCE, suggest that Cleon took legal measures against Aristophanes for his portrayal of Cleon in *Men and Their Horses* as well. Again, his suit was not successful enough to get Aristophanes to back off; Cleon was, yet again, the focus of direct attacks in *Wasps* in 422.

Aristophanes had an immediate purpose in his attack on Cleon in *Men and Their Horses*, which was to besmirch his reputation so thoroughly that he would not be elected to the position of general for which he was running. General (*strategos*, in Greek) was the most prestigious fully elected office in Athens; each of Athens' ten tribes voted annually for its general, who would serve as one of the city's main military commanders in war and advocate for the tribe when he was not in battle. While Cleon was very influential in Athens starting in 429 BCE, he exerted that influence initially outside of public office, taking advantage of the Athenian democratic system that allowed any citizen to speak to the whole assembled citizenry at the meetings of the assembly of citizens held roughly every ten days.

Did Aristophanes succeed? No. Cleon was elected general not just in 424, but also in 423 and 422. It was in this last year that he was killed while leading a losing effort against a Spartan force in a battle at Amphipolis, in northern Greece.

HISTORICAL CONTEXT

The battle between the two personalities took place in the context of a decades-long (431-404 BCE) military conflict, referred to by the Athenian historian, Thucydides, as the Peloponnesian War, that matched Athens and its allies against Sparta and its allies. That war began largely due to Sparta's concerns about Athens' ongoing expansion of its influence around the Mediterranean region.

The war had not been easy on Athens. Its military strength was in its navy, while Sparta's was in its land forces, so Athens decided to rely on sea power over land engagement, with some local consequences. Shortly after the war's inception, Pericles, a long-time general of his tribe and the most influential person in Athens' democracy for decades, convinced the Athenian people that the best way to win the war was to leave the farmland outside of the city's walls undefended, and to ship in all of the food and other resources that the city needed. The many Athenians living in the countryside were summoned to live within the walled city, and the public health consequences were severe. Between 429 and 426 BCE, a plague hit Athens in two waves, and roughly a third of the populace was killed, including, in 429, Pericles himself.

DEMAGOGUES' RISE TO POWER

This opened the door for others to fill some of the leadership void in the city. A number of those who took advantage of the opportunity were a somewhat different sort of politician than Pericles and the others who had preceded him and vied with him. The members of this new group, eventually called "demagogues" (a Greek word first attested in this very play!), have been lumped together based on the following characteristics: their families' rise to wealth in the generation before the demagogues, from business earnings based on the labors of enslaved people; their flamboyance as speakers in the Athenian assembly, where any citizen was free to address the gathered citizens; and their attention to the financial wellbeing of common Athenians, at the expense of the so-called "demagogues'" peers in wealth.

Cleon was the most successful of the early demagogues. In addition to the traits of demagogues noted in the previous paragraph, he appears also to have had a knack for convincing individual common Athenians to feel a connection of friendship with him, which helped him to cultivate a very loyal following. By taking advantage of the common ancestry that he shared with Athens' majority, and through his apparent willingness to gather in close proximity with common Athenians, he seems to have convinced a considerable number of Athens' socioeconomic underclass that they were his political circle, as politicians had always had their own political friends and allies upon whom they relied. Before Cleon, though, those political friends and allies had overwhelmingly been wealthy and from prominent families.

CLEON'S OTHER TALENT

While Cleon was a persuasive politician and astute cultivator of underappreciated supporters, he also proved to be an effective military general. In 425 BCE, an Athenian general named Demosthenes had trapped a Spartan force on the island of Sphacteria, off the coast of Pylos in western Greece. Sparta proposed a treaty that would allow it to withdraw those troops, but Cleon successfully urged the Athenian people to reject the offer. That proved to be an increasingly unpopular decision. While upholding its blockade, the Athenian force struggled to withstand attacks by other Spartans and to maintain supply chains that kept the soldiers appropriately provisioned as winter was approaching.

When these concerns were discussed in the Athenian assembly, Cleon asserted, baselessly, that the reports from Pylos were inaccurate, and that the fault lay with Athens' generals, who should have been able to manage the situation better. One such general, Nicias, offered to let Cleon take his spot and bring an expeditionary force to Pylos to check out the situation for himself. While Cleon clearly was not expecting to have to put his money where his mouth was, the assembled citizens encouraged this arrangement boisterously enough that Cleon had little choice but to accept Nicias' offer. To save face, since he figured that he would find the situation actually *was* as grim as was reported, and since he knew that many of the assembled citizens supported this expedition only to see him fail, he boasted that he would defeat the notoriously ferocious land-fighting Spartans on Sphacteria within twenty days.

To nearly everyone's surprise, Cleon, along with Demosthenes, benefitting from some turns of good fortune, presided over a plan of attack that led to the killing of 128 Spartan hoplites and the surrender of 292 more. And he did it within twenty days. For this, the Athenian people voted him the honor of free meals in the Prytaneum, the building designated for the executives (*prytaneis*) of each year's council, along with Athens' Olympic champions and others who had done great service to the city-state.

THE PLAY'S PERFORMANCE CONTEXT

Aristophanes, as noted above in "Aristophanes and His Purpose in *Men and Their Horses*," did not succeed in his ostensible political purpose for this play, in keeping Cleon from riding his wave of popularity to reelection as general. However, the play's contemporaneous engagement is typical of the comic genre of fifth-century Athens that came to be labeled "Old Comedy" (to distinguish it from evolutions of this type of comedy, which, creatively, have been labeled "Middle Comedy" and "New Comedy"). Political figures were regularly pilloried in such plays, as were other prominent public figures, artists, and actions. Aristophanes' *Clouds*, for instance, mocks the philosopher Socrates so thoroughly that Plato later cited the play's deleterious impact on Socrates' reputation during the court case against him that led to his death. Aristophanes' *Women at the Thesmophoria* playfully ridicules the work of the tragic poet Euripides. Dissatisfaction with the seemingly unending Peloponnesian War was also a common topic, appearing in such plays of Aristophanes as *Peace* and *Lysistrata*. Comic poets during this period clearly saw their role as to encourage the thousands of citizens in the audiences of their plays to consider critically all sorts of features and figures of contemporaneous Athens, to push for the best possible outcomes for the city.

As with all of the comic plays from ancient Athens of which we have substantial remains, *Men and Their Horses* was originally performed in one of Athens' two great theater festivals. *Men* was produced at the Lenaea (offered in January of each year), while others of Aristophanes' plays were initially performed at the City Dionysia (in March or April). While Dionysus, god of the theater, was the main honorand of each festival, each also offered prestigious prizes for the writers of the comedy and tragic tetralogy judged best.

In the year prior, comic playwrights applied to be among the five chosen for each festival to receive public funding to write the plays and spend months producing them. Actors and chorus members, too, received public wages for the months that they put into their preparation for their parts.

While Aristophanes won the prize for best comedy for *Men and Their Horses*, this was a rare honor for him. Despite the recognition of his plays' excellence through the millennia since then, and despite having contributed at least forty plays to these competitions (of which eleven remain), he appears to have won first prize at these festivals only three other times: at the City Dionysia in 427 for *Babylonians*, and at the Lenaea for *Acharnians* in 425 and *Frogs* in 405.

NORMS AND STRUCTURES OF ATHENIAN COMIC PLAYS

In its original performance, *Men and Their Horses* would have done several things that are typical of its genre but out of step with today's dramatic performances. For one, it would have used only three actors to play all of the individual speaking roles of the play, with each actor playing up to three different roles. To keep their various roles straight to the audience, these actors would have worn not only costumes which they changed to signify their different characters, but also masks. These static masks, made of wood or linen, designed and painted to convey a critical impression of the character they represented, were standard for all performers, other than the *aulos* (a two-piped flute) player who accompanied the chorus' songs. Also, the actors, chorus members, and everyone else involved in the production would have been men, whether the roles they played were those of men or women.

The chorus was idiosyncratic to its time as well. At the time that *Men and Their Horses* was performed, the comic choruses had twenty-four members, whose jobs were to sing and dance in unison during plays and to respond to other characters' speech during dialogue, sometimes as a group, sometimes singly, and sometimes with just the chorus leader speaking for the group. Comic choruses represented groups that fit with themes of each play, but often humorously. Wasps, birds, and clouds were among the groups that the choruses represented, with those groups having the plays titled for them (i.e., plays titled *Wasps*, *Birds*, and *Clouds*).

This play, too, is titled for its chorus. The original play was titled *Hippeis* in Greek, which translates literally to *Knights*. The title of this translation, *Men and Their Horses*, is a way for the play's translators to make the more literal translation of the play's name more accessible to a contemporary audience, which—if it thinks of knights at all—thinks of them as wearing shining armor and jousting at Renaissance faires. The Greek word *hippeis*, like the English word "knights," means, at its root, someone who operates from a horse, and typically a horse that the operator owns. Thus, in this translation, the chorus of "men and their horses" is converted to "cowboys."

The script of *Men and Their Horses* also uses the same broad organizational structures of all Athenian Old Comedies during the fifth century BCE. A *prologue*—speech or dialogue by one or more characters before the chorus' entry—sets the scene: Demosthenes and Nicias have a boss, Guy Demos, who has hired a manipulative, unscrupulous new employee, Drumpf, who has been making the two initial staffers' lives difficult, so Demosthenes and Nicias try to cultivate a rival, Hot Dog Man, to take Drumpf's spot (*Men*, lines 1-246). Then the chorus enters and speaks (it can also sing during this entrance, as it does in other comedies), in a stretch called the *parodos*; it also criticizes Drumpf for his selfishness and dishonesty (247-277). The next stretch is a debate between characters on opposing sides of an issue, called the *agon*; here, Drumpf and Hot Dog Man each argue for their greater suitability to serve Guy's interests (expressed in terms of each one being a better "lover" to Guy), with the Chorus, Demosthenes, and Nicias supporting Hot Dog Man's cause (278-497). The individual actors then leave the stage, and the chorus is left to address the audience directly about matters of the day in a stretch called the *parabasis*; here, the chorus of cowboys expresses the poet's sympathy with their cause, speaks of the difficulty of producing winning comedy as tastes change, and notes its affinity with previous generations of accomplished Athenians (498-610). An *episode* follows, in which characters and the chorus interact to take next steps concerning issues brought up in the *agon*; here, Drumpf, Hot Dog Man, and Hot Dog Man's partisans continue to make the case for themselves/ their candidate as the more suitable "lover" to Guy (611-1263). The chorus again directly addresses the audience regarding contemporary issues; in this case, the members justify publicly scrutinizing those who have achieved prominence and speak in the voice of ships who would not want certain figures to steer and ride them (1264-1315). The play concludes with an *exodos*, in which the issues raised in the rest of the play are brought to a comically satisfying resolution; here, Guy has returned to the way he used to be when Athens was at its best, and he realizes he has been manipulated and abused by Drumpf (1316-1372).

ATHENIAN PEDERASTY

One essential conceit of this play is that two men, Drumpf and Hot Dog Man, are trying to get Guy to choose them as Guy's lover. This fits (intentionally awkwardly, in this case) into the Athenian system of pederasty, in which an adult man establishes a romantic relationship with a teenage boy. There are benefits for each party: the adult man gets to enjoy the company of a young man perceived to be at the height of his attractiveness, and the teenager gets to learn from the elder and to develop a network of friends who will serve his purposes when he himself enters into adult society. There were typically restrictions on the sorts of interactions allowed between these couples: while the teenage partner (*eromenos*) could provide some sexual gratification to the adult partner (*erastes*), this was not supposed to include physical penetration, though records from the ancient world indicate that such penetration between such partners did indeed happen.

Pederasty in *Men and Their Horses* is awkward on a few levels. One of them is that Guy is clearly not a teenager, so this relationship would have struck Athenians as humorously deviating from pederastic norms. Another is that, as you will see from the accompanying notes, Drumpf appears to be quite a bit less sexually passionate in his pursuit of Guy than Hot Dog Man does. Hot Dog Man is portrayed quite sexually, in a variety of ways, as is appropriate for someone romantically pursuing someone else. But Drumpf's language and actions are much more like those of a friend. This is quite possibly because Aristophanes was portraying Drumpf in a way that would be familiar to Athenians: as someone who staked his political career on being a friend and ally to members of the lower class. There was no social institution of serving as someone's sole "super-friend," while there was one for being someone's sole pederastic lover, and other politicians had used the pederasty model to express the feelings of a leader toward those led. So Aristophanes appears to have adapted Drumpf's friendly relationship with Athenians to pederasty, but muted Drumpf's expression of it in order to pick up on what Drumpf really *did* say and do toward common Athenians.

NOTES ON THIS TRANSLATION'S ADAPTATION OF ATHENIAN OLD COMEDY TO 21ST-CENTURY AMERICA

This translation, as you will see, adapts the play in several ways from its original form to speak to its contemporary audience. One of those ways is its title and the choral performers to whom that title refers, as initially addressed in the "Norms and Structures of Athenian Comic Plays" section. The implication in the choice of "knights" as the chorus in the original version of this play is that horse ownership in classical Athens implied substantial wealth, class identification in terms of that wealth, and points of view and loyalties that often came along with that wealth and class status. These wealthy people, in Athens at the time of the play's production, had serious concerns about how demagogic politics downplayed their interests. So the chorus of "cowboys" in this play speaks from the perspective of this class of wealthy Athenians.

Other adaptations in the translation also work to make the significant concern in the original play of what to do about the political clout wielded by the Athenian lower classes and the demagogic politicians who appealed to them more understandable to contemporary readers. "Guy Demos," in this translation, represents the Athenian lower classes. In the original, he was named just *Demos*, which would have been understood as "The People," "The Common People," or, more pejoratively, "The Masses." Giving him the name "Guy" here communicates the idea of the character as a "Regular Guy." The attitude communicated by the play is that the lower classes are going to dictate Athenian policy, now that demagogues (Drumpf and Hot Dog Man) have figured out how to mobilize them; the key is to find a way to guide them so that they best serve the interests of the wealthy (personified by the "cowboys") as well.

"Hot Dog Man" is a close adaptation of the original name *Allanto-poles*, literally "Sausage-Seller." The idea in both the original and in this translation is of someone who vends a low-priced, widely available, phallically-shaped meat product. Outside of Chicago, Milwaukee, and a small number of cities with similar ethnic demographics, hot dogs fit that description in the U.S. better than sausages do.

The other, far more substantial way in which this play adapts to contemporary circumstances is in making a play which focuses on the first great Athenian demagogue into one focusing on the most prominent current American demagogue. The main character in the original play is named Paphlagon, but the play makes it clear that that character was standing in for Cleon. One way to make prominent Athenians seem illegitimate was to imply that they had recent foreign ancestry, meaning that they were not genuinely eligible for citizenship (citizenship required that both parents be full Athenians). The name "Paphlagon" implies that the figure had roots in Paphlagonia (on the southern coast of the Black Sea in Asia Minor, modern Turkey), as there were accusations that Cleon's mother did. This translation of the play turns "Paphlagon" into "Drumpf," the name that Donald Trump's patrilineal ancestors changed to the current family name sometime between the 17th and 19th centuries, but which has been much played up during Trump's presidency and the campaign leading up to it. As you will read, Trump and Cleon have plenty in common, beyond their families' foreign origins—real or imagined—being in the minds of at least some of the public.

OTHER RESOURCES

There is much more to know about Aristophanes' *Knights*, Athenian comedy, and Athenian demagogues. Here are a few sources to which interested parties could look for more information on those topics.

Dugdale, Eric. *Greek Theater in Context.* Cambridge: Cambridge University Press, 2008.

Edmunds, Lowell. *Cleon,* Knights *and Aristophanes' Politics.* Lanham, MD: University Press of America, 1987.

Henderson, Jeffrey, ed., intro., and comm. *Aristophanes: Knights.* Oxford: Oxford University Press, forthcoming.

—. ed., trans., intro., and notes. *Acharnians. Knights.* Vol. 1 of *Aristophanes.* Loeb Classical Library. Cambridge: Harvard University Press, 1998.

Hershkowitz, Aaron. "Rise of the Demagogues: Political Leadership in Imperial Athens after the Reforms of Ephialtes." PhD diss., Rutgers University, 2018.

Simmons, Robert H. *Demagogues, Power, and Friendship in Classical Athens: Leaders as Friends in Euripides, Aristophanes, and Xenophon.* London: Bloomsbury, 2022.

Sommerstein, Alan H., ed., transl, and notes. *Aristophanes: Knights.* Warminter: Aris and Phillips, 1981.

Storey, Ian. C., and Arlene Allan. *A Guide to Ancient Greek Drama.* 2nd ed. n.p.: Wiley Blackwell, 2014.

ROBERT HOLSCHUH SIMMONS

MEN *and their* HORSES

SCENE: *A neoclassical house painted white, but which saw its best days in previous generations. A less than charitable resident might even describe it as a "dump." DEMOSTHENES bursts out. Were things other than they are, he would be a respected senior staffer, but as things are in Athens, he is more like an abused gopher.*

DEMOSTHENES
Ay-yi-yi! The HORROR! The HORROR! Ay-yi-yi!
A horrible Drumpf, nouveau-bought.[1]
The gods should destroy him and his plans HORRIBLY.
From the minute he came into the house
He's been jerking around, spanking his staff.

> **NICIAS** *bursts out, equally distressed, and likewise an abused staffer, except with a touch of paranoid wimpiness, too.*

NICIAS
Most HORRIBLE indeed! Humpty Drumpty deserves a great Fall/Him, his con-jobs and all.

DEMOSTHENES
You poor schmuck. How you doing?

NICIAS
HORRIBLY. Same as you.

DEMOSTHENES
Come here for a second
So we can double our displeasure and sing a dismal dirge!

NICIAS & DEMOSTHENES *(arms locked, clinging to each other, swaying)*
Sad ... Sad ... Sad ... Sad ... Sad. 10

DEMOSTHENES *(breaking abruptly away of what could have, in theory, gone on forever)*
Wait—why are we just singing protest songs? Shouldn't the two of us
Seek some solution and cease this symphonic suffering?

NICIAS
What's our option?

DEMOSTHENES
You tell me!

NICIAS
No, you go first,
And I'll go after you.

31

DEMOSTHENES
God help me, no!
I won't!
YOU be bold and speak up, THEN I'll tell you what I think.

NICIAS
Be bold?
That sure doesn't sound like me. Perhaps instead
I could say something uber-tragilistically clever?
He poses dramatically to better pass the buck.
"How might thou sayest for me what I needest to say?"[2]

DEMOSTHENES
Enough! Quit it! Stop yanking my carrot.
Find us some way to get the fuck away from this master.   20

> **NICIAS** *ruminates while* **DEMOSTHENES** *stares piercingly.*
> *Then* **NICIAS**, *a brilliant idea coming to him, commands* **DEMOSTHENES**.

NICIAS
Ok. Say "let" then "scum," and melding your syllables together.

DEMOSTHENES
Alright I will: "Let's come."

NICIAS
Ok, next
Say "out" and "a heir" before "Let's come"

DEMOSTHENES
"Outta here."

NICIAS
Well done.
Now, do it as if you were jerking off. Start gently.
"Outta here!" then "Let's come!" Then add pressure and speed.

DEMOSTHENES
Outta here! Let's come! Outta here let's come! Let's come outta here!

NICIAS
There.
Didn't that feel good?

DEMOSTHENES
Oh god yes! Except for the skin
I'm afraid o' fore skin.

NICIAS
What's the problem?

DEMOSTHENES
Because staff who jerk off and escape have their skins peeled.

NICIAS
Then given the situation, best option for the two of us   30
Is to go and get ourselves some y' olde tyme religion.

DEMOSTHENES
Like Ancient Greek religion? Do you really believe any of it?

NICIAS
I surely do.

DEMOSTHENES
What proof do you have?

NICIAS
Well, the gods hate my guts. Isn't that proof enough?

DEMOSTHENES
Fair enough. I'll accept that. Let's switch gears.
Should I explain the plot to the audience now?

NICIAS
Can't hurt. But let's ask them for a favor.
They should make it completely clear to us, by the looks on their faces
If they're enjoying *any* part of the show—whether it's the script
or the acting.

DEMOSTHENES (*to the audience*)
Ok. Let me explain. The two of us have a boss,   40
A cranky redneck; corn-fed, easily pissed
Mr. Guy Demos of Main Street,[3] a grouchy senior
Deaf to reason. Last November, this guy
Took on a staffer, one who skins and tans hides,[4]
A deplorable jerk and diabolical liar, a Drumpf.
So tanned he's orange. He sized up the old man, the Drumpf did.
Fell on his knees before the master,
Sucking up, "serving," flattering and bullshitting him
With random twitterings, talking like this:
"Judge just one case, Guy, sir, and relax in the bath."   50
"Suck on this, slurp on that, win this, grab that."
"You want seconds?" Then he snatches up
Whatever one of US has prepared, that dirty Drumpf,
And regifts it to the master. Just yesterday I
Rolled out a Spartan loaf and that deplorable
Sprinted by, snatched it, and presented it himself
After I was the one who rubbed it out![5]

33

He drives the rest off and doesn't permit anyone else
Access to the boss. Instead he's got a leather swatter
And he stands there at dinner flicking away the establishment. 60
He sings prophecies. Now our old boy is born again!
Once he saw what a slack-jawed yokel he had,
He applied the art of the deal: he slanders the Deep State
With obvious outright lies. And then WE become the whipping boys!
The Drumpf runs around to everyone in the house,
Blaming, bullying, taking bribes, blustering,
"You see that I got that guy whipped?
If you don't grease me, you'll be next."
And so we pay ... Otherwise, we'll be whacked
By the old man and purge eight times as much in turds. 70
So hurry up now, my friend: let's figure out
How and where the two of us can go.

NICIAS
"Coming outta here" was really the best way, my friend.

DEMOSTHENES
But there's no way to dodge the Drumpf.
He supervises everything. He's got one leg
Towering over the east coast and the other out west,
So his asshole is positioned right over the heartland.
His hands are free to grab pussy, his balls in some foreign land.

NICIAS
We'd be better off dead.

DEMOSTHENES
So let's think about that: 80
What's the most manly way to die?

NICIAS
What, the manliest way?
You can die of toxic masculinity I'm told.
I heard you can O.D. on testosterone shots.

DEMOSTHENES
Hmm. Now that we're talking about shots,
How about a few drinks?
Perhaps then we can come up with something useful.

NICIAS
Nice. Always about the booze with you.
How can a drunk come up with anything useful?

DEMOSTHENES
Really, dude? What a washed-out-wimp-whiner!
How dare you deride drink for deliberative dexterity? 90
Could you find anything more inspiring than wine?
Don't you see, when people drink, then
They get rich, successful, and win every argument,
They're lucky, good looking, they say things like, "I love you, man."
Just go get me a jug of wine, quick,
So I can flood my brain and say something clever.

NICIAS
Oh lord, then what's this drink going to do for us?

DEMOSTHENES
It'll be great: just get it and I'll lie down and prepare.
Once I'm really drunk, I'll heave all over the place
With drops of resolutions, mindlets, and thoughtsies. 100

NICIAS *goes inside and returns with a jug of wine.*

NICIAS
Whew. Lucky I didn't get caught in there
Stealing the booze.

DEMOSTHENES
Hey, tell me: what's the Drumpf doing?

NICIAS
That sleazeball was licking illicit delectables,
And now he's snoring, passed-out, sprawled on his bed.

DEMOSTHENES
Go on now, pour me a large unmixed shot
To get us started.

NICIAS
Here. Offer a toast to Lady Luck.

NICIAS *gives him a drink.*

DEMOSTHENES
Chug! Chug the good old-fashion Spirits!
Lady Luck, let this booze be my guide!
He shudders, as if possessed—and snaps out of it with an idea.

NICIAS
So please, what is it?

DEMOSTHENES
The prophecies! Right away

Go inside and steal them from the Drumpf,　　　　　　　　　110
While he's asleep.

NICIAS
Well, OK, but
I fear those spirits of yours signify luck won't be a lady tonight.

DEMOSTHENES
Come on, I'll just offer up another shot to myself
To flood my mind and spew something spiffy.

> **DEMOSTHENES** *takes another shot and shudders*
> *as it hits him while* **NICIAS** *goes inside.*

> **DEMOSTHENES** *repeats the process several more times,*
> *getting progressively drunker until* **NICIAS** *returns.*

NICIAS
Wow! The Drumpf is farting and snoring up a storm!
But that's why he didn't catch me grabbing the sacred prophecy,
The one he treasures the most.

DEMOSTHENES (*now quite smashed*)
Brilliant!
Bring it over so I can read it. And you pour me something to drink,
And hurry up! Come on, let's see. What's in here?
Holy prophecies! Give me a drink right way! Chop chop!　　　　120

NICIAS (*trying to get the paper away from* **DEMOSTHENES**)
Here. What does the prophecy say?

> **NICIAS** *provides another drink, which* **DEMOSTHENES** *slugs down.*

DEMOSTHENES
Hit me again.

NICIAS
The prophecy says to hit you again? *He doubtfully pours another shot*

DEMOSTHENES
Takes the shot and shudders
Hallelujah!

NICIAS
What is it?

DEMOSTHENES
Quick, give me another shot.

> **NICIAS** *hurriedly provides another drink, which* **DEMOSTHENES** *slugs down.*

NICIAS
He sure loves that ol' time religion!

DEMOSTHENES (*reading*)
You filthy Drumpf! That's why you were on guard all this time!
You were dreading what's in your own prophecy!

NICIAS
Why?

DEMOSTHENES
Right here it says how he's to be taken down!

> *There is a pause, as* **DEMOSTHENES** *makes it clear he is not going to give the answer 'til he has more booze. He gestures.* **NICIAS** *hurriedly provides another drink, which* **DEMOSTHENES** *slugs down.*

NICIAS
How??

DEMOSTHENES
How? Basically the prophecy says that
First there is to be a Seller of Hemp.[6]
He'll be the first to control the business of our city.   130

NICIAS
That's one seller. What's next from there? Tell me.

DEMOSTHENES
After that follows a Seller of Sheep.[7]

NICIAS
Two sellers. And what will be his fate?

DEMOSTHENES
To rule until another man more disgusting than he
Comes along. And after that, he'll be taken down.
For his successor will be a Seller of Leather, the Drumpf!
A snatcher, a screecher, with the septic sound of sewer slime.

NICIAS
So it was fated that the Seller of Sheep be taken down
By the Seller of Leather?

DEMOSTHENES
Exactly!

NICIAS
That's awful. We're doomed.
Where could we get just one more Seller?   140

DEMOSTHENES
No ... there is another. Born for the art of the deal.

NICIAS
Please, tell me: who is it?

DEMOSTHENES
You sure you want to know?

NICIAS
Hell yeah!
Pause, another shot, another shudder....

DEMOSTHENES
The one who takes him down is a ... Seller of Hot Dogs![8]

NICIAS
A hot dog man? Well, we really have hit rock bottom!
So where will we find this guy?

DEMOSTHENES
Let's look out for him.

> *The* **HOT DOG MAN** *rolls his hot dog cart on stage.*

NICIAS
Hey, here's one coming
Downtown—just as luck would have it!

DEMOSTHENES:
O most holy
Hot dog man, over here! over here! My dear, dear friend,
Step right up! The Messiah has come! You look like our city's savior!

> *The* **HOT DOG MAN** *enters the stage, pushing his hot dog cart.*

HOT DOG MAN
What is it? What are you callin' me for?

DEMOSTHENES
Over here! Come and discover   150
Just how lucky and blessed a person you are!

NICIAS
Come on now: get that cart away from him and bring him up to speed
On what the god's prophecy means for him.
I'll go inside and keep a lookout for the Drumpf.

DEMOSTHENES
All right now. First drop your load and make yourself comfortable,

> **HOT DOG MAN** *puts down his spatula, apron, etc.*

Then get down on your knees ...

HOT DOG MAN looks at him in alarm

... and pray to the gods.

> HOT DOG MAN *prostrates himself awkwardly, ass in the air, confused.*

HOT DOG MAN (*suspiciously*)
OK. What's this about?

DEMOSTHENES (*with a gesture of blessing*)
A Blessed One! A Man of Riches!
Today a nobody! Tomorrow a Superman!
Lord Duke of the Blessed Athenians!

HOT DOG MAN, not amused, starts to stand up.

HOT DOG MAN
C'mon buddy, just let me beat my meat and   160
Work my sausage. Don't mock me.

HOT DOG MAN starts to walk away.

DEMOSTHENES
You moronic meathead!

DEMOSTHENES catches up to HOT DOG MAN.

Look here!
indicating the audience
Do you see all those rows of people lined up at attention?

HOT DOG MAN
Yeah.

DEMOSTHENES
You shall be the Supreme Overlord over them all!
Ruler of the Market, the Harbor and the Assembly!
The Council you will stomp! The Generals you will strip bare!
Put 'em in jail! Lock them up! And then you'll suck cock in the oval office![9]

HOT DOG MAN
Me?

DEMOSTHENES
Yes, you! You ain't seen nothing yet!
Climb up on that cart of yours and look from there.

HOT DOG MAN climbs and stands on his cart.

Look down on all the surrounding islands.   170

39

HOT DOG MAN
I'm looking down.

DEMOSTHENES
What else? You see the trade centers and freighters?

HOT DOG MAN
Yeah.

DEMOSTHENES
So aren't you blessed bigly?
Now swing your right eyeball towards the Far East,
And then use the left to look the other way, south of the border.

HOT DOG MAN
Is that what being blessed bigly is? Being cross-eyed?

DEMOSTHENES
No, no! All that you survey is commerce at your command!
Because you, according to this prophecy here,
Are the GREATEST MAN!

HOT DOG MAN
Tell me how can I,
A hot dog vendor, become any sort of man at all?

DEMOSTHENES
Don't you get it? That's exactly why you'll be great!   180
Because you're deplorable, blue-collar, and ballsy.[10]

HOT DOG MAN
Even **I** don't think this is a great idea.

DEMOSTHENES
Oy vey. What's with you that you don't think you deserve it?
You don't have an innocent conscience, do you?
You're not secretly some elite intellectual, are you?

HOT DOG MAN
God no.
Deplorable, through and through.[11]

DEMOSTHENES
Excellent luck there.
That's a good fit for a politician.

HOT DOG MAN
Buddy, I don't even have an education,
Beyond the basics. Pretty much flunked everything but gym and lunch.

DEMOSTHENES

Schooling's the only thing that will hurt you—poorly done or no! 190
Political leadership isn't for the well-educated.[12]
Nor for men who are decent and well behaved.
It's for the ignorant who love to roll in the dirt. Please don't let
This god-given opportunity slip away from you!

HOT DOG MAN

So what does that prophecy say?

DEMOSTHENES

The gods' good will,
Just wrapped in a rather fancy and tricky riddle.
"Whensoe'er the twist-taloned leather not-bald eagle shall
Snatch in his snout the stupid sanguineous sipping serpent,
Then shall the deep-fried lardy humpf of the Drumpf fall,
And on the sausage slingers will the god bestow great glory, 200
If indeed they should select the sausage-selling-less road."

HOT DOG MAN

So what's that got to do with me? Explain it to me.

DEMOSTHENES

Well, the "Leather Not-Bald Eagle" is the Drumpf right over there.

HOT DOG MAN

What are the twisting talons?

DEMOSTHENES

Self-explanatory.
He snatches things and carries them off in his crooked clutches.

HOT DOG MAN

What's with the serpent?

DEMOSTHENES

That's completely clear.
The serpent is long, sometimes a foot-long. So is a hot dog.
The snake dwells in a hole, whereas the hot dog's best between buns
So it says that the snake will conquer the
Leather Not-Bald Eagle, should he not go flaccid in his ...
Oral articulation. 210

HOT DOG MAN

That article makes my pecker twitch! But I'm just amazed
That I have the right stuff to govern the people.

DEMOSTHENES

No problem at all: you just keep doing you.
Mash and grind all business into a big hot mess,

And sweeten up the people
With nice, gooey talking points.
You have what you need for popular leadership[13]:
An annoying voice, you're tasteless and low-class.[14]
You have everything you need for a life in politics,
And the voice of scripture confirms it.   220
Now buck up and say a prayer to the patron saint of morons
So you can make THAT man (*indicating the* DRUMPF *inside*) PAY!

HOT DOG MAN
But who'll be the supporters on my side?
The rich are scared of him
and the poor fart with fear.

DEMOSTHENES
The good ol' cowboys! There's a thousand of 'em.
They hate him and they'll help you,
And all the best and the brightest citizens,
All the theater goers with a bit of sense
And then there's me, and God will be our co-pilot!
The soundstorm of a rampaging DRUMPF, *swearing and blustering.*
(*aside to the audience*)
Fear not: it doesn't really look like you-know-who.   230
The costume designers were too terrified to
Make his mask too realistic. But everyone will
Recognize him. We have smart spectators here.[15]

NICIAS
Oy! God help us. The Drumpf is coming out!

The DRUMPF *indeed arrives.*

DRUMPF
Glory to the Twelve Gods of Olympus!
Focusing on DEMOSTHENES *and the* HOT DOG MAN.
YOU, you've rigged the system against the people!
What are you drinking? Cheap foreign crap! Athens first!
You're weakening Athenian influence abroad!
You're sick and disgusting! Losers! Sad!

The HOT DOG MAN *nervously goes to his cart to depart and resume his normal business.*

DEMOSTHENES (*to the* HOT DOG MAN)
Hey you! Why are you running away? Stay here!   240
Most noble hot dog vendor, don't betray our cause!
Cowboys, stand beside us! Now is the time!
(*The* CHORUS *enters and individuals start taking the positions where they will*

42

sing their first song.)
Rangers of the Regiment, assume your positions!
The cavalry is literally here! Gallop! Canter! Present arms!
(*The* CHORUS *assemble asynchronously from* DEMOSTHENES' *orders.*)
(*to the audience*)
From all the dust, I think we're surrounded!
(*to the* CHORUS)
Charge! Chase! Make him retreat!

CHORUS
Strike the scum! Strike the scum! Smack the deplorable horse wrangler!
You pit and precipice of pilfery! Reverse Robin Hood!
IRS flunkie! You bottom-feeding chasm of the canyon!
Deplorable among deplorables!
Let me repeat that:
He was deplorable[16] all the live-long day!   250
Smack 'im! Git 'im! Hit 'im up! Run 'im down!
He's a troll him! Like we are! Make 'im holler!
Make sure he doesn't hoof it outta here!
To make a break for the bush.

DRUMPF (*to the audience*)
Gentlemen of the jury, Brethren of the Order of
Tax Cuts, whom I feed regularly with tweets,
Both honest and dishonest, HELP ME!
I'm being beaten by a Deep State conspiracy!

CHORUS
Darn tootin'! You slug and guzzle revenue
Out of office, draining the swamp into yer own pockets.
Squeezing the lemons of all government workers,   260
Seeing who gives you lemonade, who's a sourpuss.
And you snoop out citizens fitting to be fleeced.
You find someone rich, not yet corrupt, petrified in public,
And if he's mindin' his own business like some slack jaw,
You start husking his corn, slapping him with slander,
Then you hump him up on your shoulder and body-slam him good.

DRUMPF
Are you piling on me too? My good men, I'm taking the beating FOR you,
Because I was about to say that the right thing for the city to do
Is erect a monument in honor of your manliness.

CHORUS
You rodeo clown! Yer nothin' but snake-oil! You see him sneaking under
Us like we're senile, trying to doubletalk?   270
Well, if he pulls that off, he'll get stuck on this!
(gesturing between his legs)
And if he leans up here, he'll hump up my legs.
(indicating the side of his legs)
Heh, he can try to handle it but he can't!

DRUMPF *(After yearning to make the exact motions that the* **CHORUS**
expressed, he addresses the audience.)
My city! My people! I'm getting sucker punched by these thugs!

HOT DOG MAN
So you're screeching like when you try 'n' lord it over the city?

DRUMPF
I'll dominate you with my all-powerful yelling!

CHORUS (*to the* **DRUMPF**)
Yeah, if yelling was a thing, you'd be Old Yeller.
But if HE (*indicating the* **HOT DOG MAN**) whups your behind in shame-
lessness,
Then WE take the cake.

DRUMPF
I expose this man and I declare that he's engaged in a
rack-et to make cont-rack-ts with the enemy!

HOT DOG MAN
I expose HIM for running to the Capitol   280
With an empty gut and scampering out full.[17]

DEMOSTHENES *(siding with the* **HOT DOG MAN**)
I swear by god, he was embezzling his contraband, the daily bread with
much pork,
and got more slice than any politician ever before.

DRUMPF
You are both so dead.

HOT DOG MAN
I'll triple-scream you!

DRUMPF
I'll over-shout you.

HOT DOG MAN
I'll double down on screaming!

DRUMPF
I'll smear you, if you fight back.

HOT DOG MAN
I'll slap you like a bitch.

DRUMPF
I'll twitter you down to a nub.   290

HOT DOG MAN
I'll blockade your back alleys.

DRUMPF
Look me in the eye and say that.

HOT DOG MAN
I played chicken in the backstreets, too, you know.

DRUMPF
If you even peep, I'll cut you.

HOT DOG MAN
If you blabber a bit, I'll shit-can you.

DRUMPF
I'm the best at stealing. Not you.

HOT DOG MAN
With everyone looking,
I can steal their eyeballs out of their sockets.

DRUMPF
You stole that trick.   300
I'll alert the officials
about dodging the taxes
from your hot doggery.

CHORUS (*inspired by the Grinch song*)
You're a mean one, and you humpf,
you sleazy, squeamy scumbag.
Your hubris fills the earth.
You have rattled the assembly,
the tax codes, the investigations, and the courts.
You go raking up the dirt,
You mudraking extraordinaire!
Mr. Drumpf,
At a town hall meeting, we're on psycho alert.
And Athens lost its hearing when you
shouted loudly, and I quote,
"I'm

a
hunk."

DRUMPF (*back to regular speech*)
I recognize skin-tight leather when I see it.

HOT DOG MAN
Oh yeah, you know leather like I know hot dogs.
You used to make leather boots so cheap and flimsy
Just to dupe the hicks,
so that by the end of the day they were flip-flops!

DEMOSTHENES
Oh god he did that to me. My friends and neighbors   320
Laughed so hard at me when I showed up
In the 'burbs in Nike imitation sandals.

CHORUS (*inspired by "Old Town Road"*)
(*to* **DRUMPF**)
Talk down, up-town, livin' like an old czar,
Spend a lot of money on a brand new big wall,
Athens gotta have it: Persian rings and Spartan hoplites
Immigrants in cages, son of Hippodamus just cries.
But no stress. We're now through with you.
He's like an Oscar Meyer Man, time to barbeque.   330
(*to* **HOT DOG MAN**)
Since you just roll on an unethical code
School 'im back 'til he can't no more.
'cuz
Can't nobody tell 'im nothin'
You can't tell 'im nothin'

HOT DOG MAN
Listen here to what kind of "citizen" this man is!

> *They both rush to the stage door and get stuck in the door frame.*

DRUMPF
Isn't it my turn?

HOT DOG MAN
Hell no! That's the kind of deplorable[18] I am.

DEMOSTHENES
If he doesn't go for that trick, tell 'em you fell from a deplorable family
tree, too.

They wriggle out of the door frame. As **DRUMPF** *tries to rush in,* **HOT DOG MAN** *trips him and holds on to his foot.*

DRUMPF
My turn! My turn!

HOT DOG MAN
Hell no.

DRUMPF
Hell yes!

HOT DOG MAN
Hell no, damn it!
First and foremost, I'll fight for the right to be first and foremost!

They continue struggling with each other to get to the door.

DRUMPF
Urrrrgh, I'm dying up here!

HOT DOG MAN
Uh uh. I won't let you!   340

DEMOSTHENES
Let him! Let him! Please, let the man die up here!
They warily release each other and stand watching each other, in case
one makes a mad dash for the door.

DRUMPF
What makes you think that you have the right to slander me?

HOT DOG MAN
Cuz I can talk and cook shit up just like you.

DRUMPF
You? Talk? You'd be OK if a speech plopped in your lap all raw and
uncooked … you'd handle your meat like a champ. You know what I
think your deal is? Same as most people: if you come up with a slogan
against some little illegal immigrant, after having pounding it out the
night before and muttering it to yourself in the streets, pounding water, you regurgitate it for everyone, and piss off your friends.
THEN you think you are a powerful speaker! You moron. Ignorant
dumbass.   350

HOT DOG MAN *(now forceful and articulate)*
Yeah, what are *you* drinking that convinced you that the city should
submit to your singular tongue lashing and lie there silent?

DRUMPF
You compare me to a mere human? I'll gulp down raw meat, guzzle the
hard stuff, and then make the Fake News my real bitch.[19]

HOT DOG MAN

Well I can chow down on fried bacon, grease, and lard, and then without washing, I'll deep throat the politicians and make the wimps cringe.

DEMOSTHENES

I liked what you said, except for that one part doesn't sit with me,
where you slurp up the porky political overflow all by yourself.   360

DRUMPF

Ha, you're not gulping down bowls of border baste and then walling
them off!

HOT DOG MAN

But I am preparing one hell of a military BBQ!

DRUMPF

I'll jump up on the City Council and freak them the fuck out.

HOT DOG MAN

I'll stuff your butthole like it's a true sausage party.[20]

DRUMPF

I'll drag you outside face down and ass up!

DEMOSTHENES

Well then, by god, if you're going to drag him, I want to go in drag too!

DRUMPF

I'll lock you up, bigly!

HOT DOG MAN

I'll indict you as a coward.

DRUMPF

I'll beat you 'til your skin is black, blue, and orange!

HOT DOG MAN

I'll stuff my loot in your sack!   370

DRUMPF

You'll spread 'em and get pegged on the ground.

HOT DOG MAN

I'll grind you like hamburger.

DRUMPF

I'll pluck off your eyebrows.

HOT DOG MAN

I'll rip your twittering throat out.

DEMOSTHENES

By God then we'll shove an apple in his mouth like master chefs do,
then grab his tongue, inspect it   380

with his asshole—I mean, mouth—gaping open—to see how poisoned
it is.

By this point, it is **DRUMPF** *against the world, or at least the other characters
on stage, but he confidently holds his own. Despite the numerical imbalance, the*
CHORUS *feels the need to declare their position, with a touch of hominess.*

CHORUS
I heard the speeches in my town,
Shameful all around
Horrible sound
Heat a fire and burn it down.
Ridin' on a horse, ha
You can whip his arse
Twirl like a twistee
You can beat him with your grip, now.
I'm gonna ride my horse up the Athens road,
I'm gonna squeeze 'til he cries, "No more!"
If you launch into him, soften him up, you'll find him a coward. I know
his ways.   390

HOT DOG MAN
That's him alright, been that way all his life.
He pretends to be a real man, profiting from another's crops.
Wants to keep all the amber waves of grain
Locked up in a silo, just for his own profits.

DRUMPF
I'm not afraid of you: the City Council thrives
with slack-jawed yokels dictating policy.

CHORUS
Hair orange, skin orange, nothing gonna tone him,
No amount of shamin' ever gonna change him,
Always got hate 'im; better loathe him
than be a bed pan,
Singing up a shitstorm in a tragicomic ku klan.   400
Flittin' 'round, he's gotta teflon tweet,
He got a bumblebee mouth so ya kick him back.
Wish I could sing a toast like an old paean,
kick ass like the Greatest Generation.
So would I sing
Once again, with pride:
You can't always get what you want!

The DRUMPF *and the* HOT DOG MAN *go to their corners like boxers preparing for the fight.*

DRUMPF

You are not going to beat me when it comes to depravity,
no way in hell! May God
banish me from the sacred rites of street-smart speechmaking first![21] 410

HOT DOG MAN

By the beatings from the boxers and the butchers with their blades
I carry the reminders of every blow that laid me down and cut me 'til I
cried out,
"I'll defeat you, I'll defeat you," if I was on table scraps sustained.

The DRUMPF *and the* HOT DOG MAN *start sparring.*
DEMOSTHENES *supports the* HOT DOG MAN.

DRUMPF

Table scraps? You can't be top dog on table scraps!
You deplorable,[22] you can't live on puppy chow and fight a son-of-a-
bitch like me!

HOT DOG MAN

Oh, hell yeah! I knew all the other tricks
When I was just a boy,
"Look there, lads!" to the butchers, I'd say,
"Springtime's come with a swallow's call!"
They'd look—and my fingering thieves snatched meat from their stall.

420

DEMOSTHENES (*to the audience*)

That's smart on the farm that is:
Grabbin' the meat before someone choked the chicken.

HOT DOG MAN

I always got away with it.
On the odd chance I was spotted, and subpoenaed
I'd shove the meat up my butthole,[23] swearing with disdain
So innocently outraged the politicians would exclaim,
"He'll be a star
He's destined for high office!"[24]

DEMOSTHENES (*to the audience*)

He got that one right,
(*to the* HOT DOG MAN)
but it's easy to see how.
You were a liar, a crook, and took meat up your ass!

DRUMPF

I'll put an end to your chutzpah—both of you! 430
I'll huff and I'll puff, breaking a mighty wind,
Rocking you babies like a hurricane!

HOT DOG MAN

And I, brandishing bravely my bratwurst in the full force gale
Shall slice my onion skin sails until you cry stormy tears!

DEMOSTHENES

And I'll make sure the juice doesn't squeeze out the boat's bottom.

DRUMPF

Never shall you abscond from our fair city
With millions and zillions!

DEMOSTHENES

Watch for the eruption of innuendo! This northeastern-er is blowing
forth impeachments!

HOT DOG MAN

We know where you russkied to get your millioniskis.

DRUMPF

Will you take 130K? That's how I normally handle such "Stormy" situations.

DEMOSTHENES *(steps in idiotically)*

The man accepts gladly! Slacken the foreskin ... I mean forward sails. 440
The winds are dying down.

DRUMPF

Ha! Now you'll face four charges for bribery!

HOT DOG MAN

You'll face twenty charges for draft-dodging and more than a thousand
for corruption!

DRUMPF

I'm calling you out: You're descended from sinners and racists!

HOT DOG MAN

And I say your grandfather saluted his leader faithfully.

DRUMPF

Faithfully? Why not?

HOT DOG MAN

Right hand out, palm up, sieg heil!

DRUMPF

Troll!

HOT DOG MAN
Deplorable!

DEMOSTHENES *encouraging the* **HOT DOG MAN**
Man up and hit him!

> **HOT DOG MAN** *starts pummeling the* **DRUMPF**.

DRUMPF
Ow! Ow! The haters are hitting me!

DEMOSTHENES *encourages the* **HOT DOG MAN**
Hit him like a real man!
Sock him in the belly
With relish and mustard jelly
'Til he pukes up his manhood.

> *The* **HOT DOG MAN** *gets the better of the punching match and the* **DRUMPF**
> *staggers away.*

CHORUS *holding up* **HOT DOG MAN'S** *hand as victor*
You handsome hunk of meat, gutsiest of all,
Your appearance meant salvation for our city, her citizens, and ourselves.
How well you have blasted this guy with your scintillating speaking.
How may we parade your praise to parallel our pleasure? 460

DRUMPF
Don't you worry, I sensed that this plot was being
Constructed against me. I just knew
There was some slimy, sticky banging going on.

HOT DOG MAN
Well I sensed what abroad he's doing now:
Talking tough on security but tweeting secrets
To our enemies—all for his own profit.

DEMOSTHENES
Oy vey! I was hoping you'd make more tool jokes.

HOT DOG MAN
I also know what the entire building is constructed upon.
I recognize its foundation and its fake real estate.

DEMOSTHENES
Awesome! You smacked his wood with hot iron! 470

HOT DOG MAN
And he's got men over there hammering everything through.

You can keep offering funds and money to me
Send your staffers around, but you won't keep me
From leaking everything I know to the people!

DRUMPF
Not before I go to the Council right now and
Tell them your conspiracy against me,
All those terrorizing plots against the country,
Conniving with those states in the middle east,
And all the scams you're brewing with our frenemies.

HOT DOG MAN
Just what are you brewing with your business frenemies, anyway?   480

DRUMPF
That's it! I'm going downtown to knock you on your ass.

The DRUMPF humpfs off stage.

DEMOSTHENES (*to the* **HOT DOG MAN**)
All right come on now! What are you thinking? Got the guts?
Teach us a lesson, if you really did stash that
Sausage up your butt, as you claim you did.[25]
Quick, run off to the capital,
Cuz he's going to burst in on them and slander
Us all as he shrieks his screams.

HOT DOG MAN
Yes, I'll go, but first I'll leave my knives and fixings here.

DEMOSTHENES (*preparing* **HOT DOG MAN** *for a "professional"*
wrestling match)
Hold on a sec. Smear this on your neck,   490
So you can slip out of his strangling slander.

HOT DOG MAN
Good idea. A real pro-wrestling trick for you!

DEMOSTHENES
Hold on now. Take these and pop 'em in your mouth.

He gives the HOT DOG MAN some suspicious looking pills.

HOT DOG MAN
What are they?

DEMOSTHENES
Something to enhance your performance in battle.
Now chop-chop, quick!

HOT DOG MAN
I'm on it.

DEMOSTHENES
Keep your eye on his balls:
Bite him! Smear him! Swallow down his cocky attitude!
And once you've pecked away his pecker, you can come back!

CHORUS (*to the* **HOT DOG MAN**)
(*inspired by "Hello Goodbye"*)[26]
Go farewell! Go succeed,
As we hope you always will, will, will!
Go, go!
The spirit of the streets will protect you.[27]
We say to you:
From us applause will be for you,
Applause for you!
For you! For you!
From us applause will be for you,
Applause for you!
Turning to the audience
As for you, won't you please
Listen up, when we sing high and low,
hey yo!
You know the songs there are to know,
You know! You know!
We trust you'll follow every verse as they will flow,
You know the flow.
We trust you'll follow every verse as they will flow,
(*inspired by "The Gambler"*)
If a man in the day,
With a gag as a decoy,
Had met up with us cowboys,
He would not have had our aid.
But we make an exception
For on this brilliant pair of dudes,
Excitement overtakes us,
So we begin to say:
We say: "Folks, these men deserve
All our praise for speaking justice,
Hatin' those that we hate,
For the way they speak what's right.
So if you don't mind us sayin',
"Y'can see it on their faces,

500

510

54

Hail Zeus for their courage,
So noble is their fight."
If you asked them a question
When you saw them, and then wondered
Why they waited for so long
On translating our play
Now they're out to fully explain
That they're not so simpleminded,
They say, when your gonna translate jokes, boy,
You gotta learn to do 'em right.
The Muses know when to tell you,
Know when to scold you,
Know when to walk away,
And know when to pun.
You never count on Muses
When you're writing for the scholars,
Only some who write are funny,
When the scripts are done.

The fearless (?) **TRANSLATORS** *take the stage.* [28]
Every translator knows how much harder it is
To translate comedy —especially ancient comedy—
Into a modern context.
Sure, you have a sympathetic audience,
(After all, we're all east-coast liberals, aren't we?)
But at the end of the day, knowledge of Ancient Greek
Might make one a scholar, but scholars aren't necessarily
Playwrights. Nor are they necessarily funny.   520
(Often quite the contrary!)
So our translators were reluctant to step forward to translate Aristophanes,
Knowing how lame such translations can be:
Either there are weak associations between antiquity and modernity
Pounded poorly into some semblance of a joke
Or the jokes become obsolete overnight.
Or the choral hymns don't work as song parodies.
Or it's hard to find a consistent voice.
Or the parallels don't really work.
Or it's far funnier in Ancient Greek.
Or the political overtone is shrill and preachy.   530
They've seen other people attempt to modernize Aristophanes
And it often falls flat— or even if it works for the day,
The expiration date is fast approaching.
Fearing all this kept our translators dicking around.   540

They said that one should try being the rower before being the captain.
Only after being promoted to Full Professor should one try to ride storms.
After THAT one could take full charge. That's why
They had restraint, instead of leaping like lemmings
Into the slimy sea of insipid satire.
But given the world we live in nowadays,
To anachronistically paraphrase Juvenal
"It's hard NOT to want to translate Aristophanes."
Now splash, thrash, and crash your hands together
Wag your tongues and other noise-making dangly bits
For the brashest, boldest, and baldest translators of them all!   550

CHORUS
(*inspired by "The Halls of Montezuma"*)
O the horsey god Poseidon,
Who likes bronze on cloven hooves,
And favors equine whinnying,
And the battleships on sea,
Bringing money at a rapid pace,
And he likes our jockeys, too.
Whether they do win or lose,
When they race their chariots.
Do join us at our song and dance,
Golden trident and dolphin,   560
You hear prayers in every harbor port,
Ever since antiquity.
In the days of old school fighting men,
You were the god of choice for them.
You will find in Athens all of us
Love you more than anyone.
Now we desire to praise our forefathers,
Men worthy of our country and its flag.
Fighting footsoldiers and the ranks of the navy,
Victorious everywhere, bringing glory to our city.
Not a single one concerned with the enemy's numbers;   570
His heart just stood ready for defense.
If ever knocked down, he'd just stand up,
Brush that dirt off his shoulder,
And soldier on again.
No old school officer ever
Applied to a bureaucrat for a state handout,
Whereas now they won't fight without a
Lucrative retirement package. As for us, we declare

56

Our right to fight for our city and her gods.
In return we ask for but one thing:
If ever peace rules and our troubles cease,
Don't disrespect our service once we strut our stuff as civilians.   580
(*inspired by "The Halls of Montezuma"*)
City guardian Athena,
of the sacred land Athens,
which surpasses all the world,
in war and poetry,
and in power over all Greece,
Come to here and have at your side,
For the battle we will fight,
Your attendant Victory.
Our companion in our dancing song,
Who contends in every fray,
And as we stand tall battling,   590
Overcomes the enemy.
For your look and approving eye,
We do look to see your smile.
Now or never it just must be,
To achieve our Victory.
We would like to tell you why we love our horses so:
Since they surely deserve praise. So many actions
They've undertaken with us, assaults and battles.
But we're not as amazed by their derring-do on land
As the manliness of their horsey jumps into their trailer boats,
Having purchased their own flasks and fortified feed bags.   600
Then they grabbed their oars just like we mere mortals,
Leaned into it, neighing, "Yippie-ki-yay! Are you hung like a horse?"
Gotta grab it harder! Pick up the pace! Get a move on, you high class
stud!"
They stormed the beaches at Corinth. The young colts
Saddled up the tents with their hooves and foraged for feed.
Instead of consuming comestible clover they chomped on crabs,
When they crawled toward a Clydesdale or were fished out by a Friesian.
Drumpf's personal chef was even known to have heard a Corinthian
crab cry,
"One if by land, two if by sea,
I just can't escape the cavalry!"   610

HOT DOG MAN *returns.*

Ah, our favorite and most youthfully vital of men!
What a headache your absence gave us.

But now, since yer now back with us safely,
Report on your competition.

HOT DOG MAN

You might as well call me Congress Whipper!
I hooked 'em on the line like a Master Baiter!
I am the champion, my friend, because I kept on fighting to the end.

CHORUS (*to "Go Tell It on the Mountain"*)

Let the people be so happy
Holler out in their joy.
Tell all that you performed,
More than words you say.
I'd travel over long roads,   620
List'ning to you declare.
Trust speaking with your courage
You man beyond compare!

HOT DOG MAN

You sure want to hear the story I've got.
I scurried right on outta here, on the heels of ol' Drumpf,
And he was already there at the Town Square,
Thunderin' and spittin' out his fake news against the cowboys,
Manufacturing mountains of conspiratorial claptrap
Convincingly! 'n' the whole crowd was chompin' at the bit,
Cowed to the point of calamity.
I saw that they were sucking and swallowing
His spicy, sweet tall tale,   630
So I summoned all my spirit:
"Hear me now, Lord of the Players and Nay-sayers
Party Crashers, Word-Trashers and Smart-Assers
Savviness of the Streets where I was raised,
Grant me the talent to talk the talk,
To trip him and trap him with my own tattle tales."
And after I spoke, there came a sign,
Some asshole farted in response to my prayer.
I fell to my knees in deference to the Spirit,
Wiggling my butt so hard that the platform   640
Nearly splintered beneath me,
And I began to bellow:
"Citizens of our fair town, I bring good news
And I want to be the first to tell you:
Since the outbreak of the Great War,
The price of beanie weenies has fallen to an all-time low!"

You could see all those angry faces smile at that.
They were ready to pin a medal on me.
And then I told 'em, all confidential-like,
That they should start hoarding up canned beans,
And they'll have weenies for pennies on the dollar.   650
You shoulda seen 'em.
I could 'a' throwed weenies in their mouths from a block away
Their jaws had dropped so far open.
Now that Drumpf, he knew what that crowd hankers for,
So he made his appeal: "Gentlemen,
In gratitude for this bounty, in my humble opinion,
A thanksgiving BBQ offering should be provided
To our patron Lady Athena, a hundred cattle."
The folk started swingin' back his way again,
And I realized that I could get buried
Under a plop of his big ol' bull ... tweet,
So I called and raised on him: TWO hundred cattle!
And if weenies cost less than a penny,
Thanksgiving should be a thousand poultry, not a paltry one hundred. 660
The town tongues started watering in my direction again.
That old Drumpf was stuttering and slavering more than talkin' by that
time.
The sheriff and his deputies started hauling him off
And the townfolk were all abuzz about pork-n-beans.
Well he started shouting out somethin' 'bout the enemy
Being ready to end the Great War—the best treaty!
But everybody figured
That was just on account o' the cheap weenies,
So war didn't bother 'em so much. "Let 'em eat cake!"   670
They just begged the mayor and his gang to adjourn the meetin'.
Everyone started scramblin',
but I headed straightway to the general store
And bought up all the hot sauce.
Then when everybody needed a little heat for their beanie weenies,
I sweetened my deal and gave everybody a few free drops.
They LOVED me and lifted me on their shoulders,   680
And it didn't but cost me a few pennies for the hot sauce!

CHORUS (*resuming "Go Tell It on the Mountain"*)
Your success is just and worthy
As it always should be.
The Drumpf has suffered rightly,
You scum much worse than he!

With all the best words screeched out,
For the battle you prepare.
Trust us throughout as allies:
Us cowboys we declare!   690

HOT DOG MAN

Look out! Here comes the Drumpf!
Blowing hot air from both ends, stirring shit up!
He's gonna huff and he's a gonna puff,
And he's thinking he's gonna blow me down whole!
That big, bad Drumpf!

DRUMPF

I'll wreck you, so help me! If I don't have enough
Fake news to do it, I'll vanish into the void!

HOT DOG MAN

Your tweets tickle me! I laugh at your pathetic posts!
I fart in your general direction!
And I give you a double bird shot!

DRUMPF

Oh no you didn't! If I don't chew you up
And spit you out of the country, I'll die!

HOT DOG MAN

Too much to take in, am I? Even if I don't guzzle you,   700
Having to swallow even a bit of your BS makes me puke.

DRUMPF

I'm going to destroy you, I swear by my poll numbers.

HOT DOG MAN

Your poll numbers! I've got a pole for you
Right here—one that's not really good for your ratings!

DRUMPF

Lock you up! Lock you up!

HOT DOG MAN

Nasty! Here, what can I give you to put your mouth around?
What do you like? Baloney on white with a very small pickle?

DRUMPF

I'll gouge out your guts with my tiny hands!

HOT DOG MAN

I'll shred you like a colonoscopy gone wild!

DRUMPF
I'll haul you before the people and you'll get what's coming to you. 710

HOT DOG MAN
No, I'll haul YOU and slander you even more.

DRUMPF
You deplorable, the people will never trust you.
But I can shoot someone on the street anytime I want.

HOT DOG MAN
You really believe the people are all yours.

DRUMPF
I understand what really feeds the people.

HOT DOG MAN
You're like an unholy cross between a mother bird
And a tit for sale: You grab the people's economic nourishment
But you swallow and digest most of it yourself,
You just drool out leftovers to trickle down to the people's mouths.

DRUMPF
That's nothing! I know an even better trick:
The people expand and contract at my command. 720

HOT DOG MAN
Yeah, well, so does my asshole.

DRUMPF
No way, buddy, are you going to publicly diss me.
Let's go before the people! Guy himself!

HOT DOG MAN
I don't see why not!
Come on! Get going before we're obstructed!

They knock at the door of **GUY**.

DRUMPF
Hey Guy! Come on out here!

HOT DOG MAN
Come on, Guy!
Out here now!

DRUMPF
Oh dearest Guysie-wisie!
Come out to play! You have to see how they're cheating me!

GUY *emerges.*

GUY

Who's shouting? Get away from my door!
You banged my public bush to bits!
OK, Drumpf, who's after you now?   730

DRUMPF

I'm taking a beating
By this … dude, and a bunch of punks, all for you.

GUY

Why?

DRUMPF

Because I love you, my Guy.
I wanna be your man.[29]

GUY (*to* **HOT DOG MAN**)

And you? Who are you?

HOT DOG MAN

I'm more your lover than he is.
I've yearned for you for so long, wanting to do good things to you, my
Guy,
Just like many other decent, proper individuals.[30]
But we can't, because of HIM.
You're like a bunch of dreamy-eyed teenage girls
You're not interested in the sweet, nice boys.
Instead you throw yourself at the greaseball gas station guys,
The dopey jocks, gun-toting criminals, the wealthy douchebags.   740

DRUMPF

Because I treat my Guy right.

HOT DOG MAN

Tell me: how do you do that?

DRUMPF

Really? I stepped in, made the country great again,
And now we're always winning and employment is up!

HOT DOG MAN

That's like taking credit for making a factory great again
By sneaking in and stealing a worker's lunchbox.

DRUMPF

Let's take this straight to the people!
Hold a town hall and let people decide which of us
Is the most biddable and beddable.[31]
Bestow your electoral love on the winner.

HOT DOG MAN
Yes, yes, decide on the winner.
Just don't use your social networks.

GUY
I won't even consider other media outlets! 750
For me, social networks are the only thing I hear.

HOT DOG MAN
Oh god, now I'm screwed.
The people normally are perceptive
and act in their own self-interest.
But once he's tangled up in that web.
His social network makes him a complete goober.

CHORUS (*inspired by "The Devil Went Down to Georgia"*)
Hot Dog Man, power up your phone and lock your network feed.
'Cause hell's broke loose in Athens, and the Drumpf'll scream his screed.
And so to win, you need to master viral media
But if you lose, the Drumpf'll rule the law.
Take aim now, boy. It's time to lock and load.
And get ready to drop your load on HIM. 760

DRUMPF
I pray to Lady Liberty, queen of our city,
that if I have been a dependable public servant
On par with the other demagogues, sleaze-balls, and whores.
May I continue to reside in the Oval Office,
By defunding, I mean defending, the majority.
If I hate you, the Athenian People, if I am not
Your truest public servant, may I be chained
In leather but not whipped, if you get my drift.[32]

HOT DOG MAN
Let me tell you, the People,
If I don't love and adore you,
May I be stuffed and boiled in a wiener sack. 770
And if that's not enough for you,
Heat my buns, grind me into a royale with cheese,
And drag me by my balls to Boot Hill with a meat-hook.[33]

DRUMPF
Well, let ME tell you, no one LOVES you more than I do.[34]
In my business, I knew how to make a profit,
Worked with small businesses,
and I knew
How to say "You're fired!" with no favoritism.

While he wants you with him, I am with you.[35]

HOT DOG MAN

That ain't worth bragging about. I can do that.
I can fire up people's buns and make you a shareholder.
He doesn't love you. He's not on your side.[36]
That's what I'm going to school you.
To him, it's all about getting his own piece of the pie
And letting you eat cake.
You were the Greatest Generation.
And scored victory after victory,[37]
But now you put up with his tongue-lashings.
He doesn't care that you're working your ass off now.
Not like me. I want your ass to relax. Have this cushion
I made for you. I don't want to see your cheeks chafed!

GUY

Dude, who are you?
You're a modern founding father, aren't you?[38]
This proves you really love your country old school.

DRUMPF

Those are terribly tiny tidbits that turn him into your token.[39]

HOT DOG MAN

More tidbits than you let trickle down to him.

DRUMPF

Hold on. If there's ever been a man
A stronger proponent for the people, who's loved you better,[40]
Shave me bald!

HOT DOG MAN

How can you say that? Love the people?[41]
They were in bunkers, trenches, and
On the front lines for years now
Without a tweet from you on their behalf.
Instead you turn a blind eye and bleed him dry!
Diplomatic chances for stability and peace
Have been blown away, spanked by
Your tyrannical executive orders.

DRUMPF

And that's what will make Athens great again.
It is manifest destiny
That the People's Court will someday rule supreme.
If they just hold on. I will be servant and provider.

I might not be innocent, but they will prosper.   800

HOT DOG MAN
You don't care about making Athens great.
You want to pursue business deals on an
International scale under the cover of the fog of war,
While the people, blinded by gloom and doom, don't see your dema-
goguery.[42]
They gape at you, distracted by debt, fear, and hope of meaningful
employment.
If Guy ever returns to the peaceful life, without the fear-mongering,
Quietly enjoying his morning oatmeal without alarms going off.
Not afraid to live by good old Athenian values,
Instead of waiting for you to build walls and bring back jobs,
Then you'll rouse the giant, they'll sprint to vote you out of office.
You know it's true, so you resort to fake news and evangelist nationalism.

DRUMPF
I cannot believe you're saying such hateful and untrue things about
me. Sad!   810
In front of all of Athens and the entire country. Fake News! After all
my great things,
Believe me! No one has done more great things than me!

HOT DOG MAN
Holy pompous comparison, Batman!
Can you believe what you're hearing? No one greater?
The founding fathers? The revolutionaries?
Those who united us all into one state?
Led us to victory through wars hot and cold?All you did was break
down Athenian unity by constructing walls
And fabricating conspiracies—you who claim to be the next great
republican
While the rest are running scared, you're grabbing greedily with your
tiny hands.

DRUMPF
I go to the people:
Isn't it disastrous that they're after me because I believe in winning? 820
Horrible!

GUY
Shut up, you shit-eating deplorable!
You've been ripping me off under my nose for years!

HOT DOG MAN
My guppy Guy, he's a swamp monster,

For all the deplorable deeds he did.
Whenever you sit there waiting, mouth agape, he's working the shaft, stroking it
With his grubby little hands and swallowing all the treasure himself.

DRUMPF
Hot Dog Man is stealing from the people! Lock him up!

HOT DOG MAN
Drumpf full of fluff.
Should be drained from the Athenian Swamp.   830
Let's make sure your corruption
Is exposed for everyone to see!

CHORUS (*to "The Devil Went Down to Georgia"*)
Now you're a proven benefactor the best mankind has,
I envy how on your tongue tip all the words they do besiege.
And you're the best around Greece, and all the control yours,
In your hand a budget memo, with all revenue streams to you.
You've got him pinned down now.
You'll win the match easily with that physique.   840

DRUMPF
Guy! Let me tell you, there's no problem.
What I've done is so great—the greatest thing ever.
It should make all those haters shut up for good.
As long as we remember my *unpresidented* election win.

HOT DOG MAN
Yeah, hold up about that win. There, you're wide open.
If you really loved the people,[43] you'd never have
Undermined whatever news source you disliked.
(*to* GUY)
It's a trap, Guy! This way, if you ever want to   850
Punish this twerp, you won't have any options.
You see the armed ranks he has around him—the rednecks,
The white trash, and the blue-collared—all rolled up into one.
So—if you were to start grumbling and looking impeachy-keen
They'd be roused against anyone trying to find proof,
Overshadowing any facts and denying access to genuine truth!

GUY
Oh lordy, daddy told me there'd be a government takeover one day
(*to* DRUMPF)
You cheatin' liar, you've been screwin' me good!

DRUMPF

Wrong! My friend, don't believe everything you hear.   860
And don't think that you can find a better friend than me.[44]
I'm the only one fighting the border crisis!
But they won't be able to keep sneaking around.
I'll expose them to you!

HOT DOG MAN

You're like weather forecasters.
Nobody watches when it's going to be nice out.
They get attention when it's storms and disasters,
So you stir up your own storms and disasters.
But tell me:
Have you ever trickled down anything to Guy here,
Who you say you love and serve—
Shelter or even a job from yourself?[45]

GUY

No, not a thing!   870

HOT DOG MAN

I'll give you the shirt off my back right now.

> **HOT DOG MAN** *puts a fresh shirt on* **GUY**.

GUY

That fits mighty nice.
You really got my back.

DRUMPF

Is one shirt all it takes? Terrible!
Look at what I did for you!
I'm the one keeping those rapists and perverts
Out of the country.

HOT DOG MAN

Oh no, you just want to corner the market on raping and perversion!
To keep those fuckers from voting against you!
You're worried bigger perverts will get into office!   880
And here's poor Guy:
At his age—without decent clothes to wear.
And winter is coming!
Here, take this suit I got.
Now you look professional.[46]

> **HOT DOG MAN** *continues improving* **GUY'S** *sartorial eloquence.*

GUY

No founding father ever found such an idea!
I mean, they came up with some amendments and declarations and all—
But this is a really nice suit!

DRUMPF

Can you believe this? Look at this monkey business you're attempting!

HOT DOG MAN

No way. Just aping your own tactics. Just like a drunk man taking a shit.
You have to use whatever comes to hand.

DRUMPF

You can't outfit me!   890
Here, Guy, try on MY suit!
(to **HOT DOG MAN***)*
Sorry, deplorable, that's the way it's gonna be.

GUY

Ugh. It smells like hell.
Like glue for orange hair.

HOT DOG MAN

That's what he's trying to do: suffocate you.
He tried to maneuver you that way before.
Remember when he promised lower prices on groceries?

GUY

Oh yeah!

HOT DOG MAN

He just wanted subsidies on pork and beans
So that at those town halls everybody would
Suffocate from the farting. [47]

GUY

You know what? Some asshole told me that. I thought he was just blowing hot air.   900

HOT DOG MAN

And didn't you all just swell up and explode? It must have stank for you!

GUY

We were all full of shit at that point, I am tellin' you.

DRUMPF

No morals at all! It's not fair to beat me with comedy! Not nice!

HOT DOG MAN

Divine will says that I should beat you at bullying.

DRUMPF

No one out-bullies me! I declare to you now, Guy,
I'll feed you a nice social bowl of security for gobbling—no strings
attached.[48]

HOT DOG MAN

I'll write you a prescription for health care
To soothe all your aches and pains.

DRUMPF

I'll barber and dye your hair, to make Athens young again!

HOT DOG MAN

I'll make sure your luck changes: no gambling at my crooked casinos!

DRUMPF

Come on, Guy, blow your nose and
Wipe the snot on my head!   910

HOT DOG MAN

NO! On mine!

DRUMPF

(to **HOT DOG MAN**)
I'll saddle you with a defense contract
And hold up the payments.
Payment will be only on delivery,
But there'll be delays and overruns
And you'll have old facilities
With no overhead covered.

HOT DOG MAN

This guy's on fire! Almost to the boiling point!
He's gonna blow!   920
Turn off the gas!
Let's hose off his threats. Use this!

DRUMPF

You'll pay for this bigly
When I smoosh you with taxes.
After all, you're not in the 1%
So you'll pay and pay and pay!

HOT DOG MAN

I'm not going to threaten you.
I'm going to use HOPE!
I HOPE you have a bucket of chicken   930
All fried and ready—just when you're
About to give a high-stakes speech,

I HOPE you cram that drumstick down,
Cause you're so pumped to crow.
Then, before you finish swallowing
May some other man come—in.
And you're so overeager for his money shot
You croak, choking on the chicken.   940

CHORUS
Amen to that, brother!

GUY
I agree.
He's lookin' to me like a right good citizen,
The likes a which ain't no one seen in ages
Supportive of all the Joe Six-Packs.
Drumpf, now you got me all riled up,
All your talk about lovin' me.[49]
Really chafes my cheeks! No more free-access
Down my passageway! It's time to change your password.[50]
You're fired!

DRUMPF
All right.
I'll tell you this, though.
The next guy will be even more deplorable.   950

GUY
Hey, my password still isn't working.
It's still something else.
(to **HOT DOG MAN***)*
Can you figure it out?

HOT DOG MAN
What was your password?

GUY
God4Athens.

HOT DOG MAN
No, that doesn't work.

GUY
What is it, then?

HOT DOG MAN
NE1469[51]

GUY
That's disgusting!

Put in my patriotic password!

DRUMPF
No, sir!
Please, not until you've heard God's secret for me. 960

HOT DOG MAN
Then listen to his plan for me, too.

DRUMPF
Hmf. If you trust him,
You'll end up with water squirted up your wineskins,
Believe me!

HOT DOG MAN
If you trust HIM,
You'll get your wineskins sucked right off,
Believe ME! [52]

DRUMPF
But I see a future where you rule the world
And sleep in a bed of roses, tired from so much winning!

HOT DOG MAN
Well, my future has you dressed like a king,
impeachy keen all the live-long day.

GUY
Well, all right, then.
(to **HOT DOG MAN***)*
You just go ahead and preach your future.
(to **DRUMPF***)*
And you, too. 970

DRUMPF
Will do.

HOT DOG MAN
I don't mind. Mine're all real. I didn't just make them up.

CHORUS
It'll be a frickin' sweet day
For those in attendance
And those just passing through,
If a certain leader of ours goes down in flames.
*(the chorus members begin chanting
"Drumpf, Drumpf, Drumpf,
Death to Drumpf"
to the tune of "Duke of Earl" while the leader speaks)*

I say this
Although down at the Diner of Discontent,
Where the Old Farts know how to Fix the Future,   980
I heard some old biddies
Goin' on 'bout how if it hadn't been for Drumpf
Becomin' such a Big Man
In our magnificent metropolis,
It would have been a double loss:
A big swinging stick and some wrecking balls.
And this, too
Is astounding to me:
In his business studies in the swine Penn,
His mates say he never liked books,   990
And refused to worm into them,
And his tutors finally threw him out,
Saying,
"He can't read the pages of any books,
He just pages bookies!"

DRUMPF (*stumbling around with his eyes closed, speaking in tongues*)
... The visions! The visions!
I can barely keep up with them!

HOT DOG MAN (*likewise, and then farts*)
... I'm so full of prophecy, it's coming out my ass.

GUY
What are y'all talkin' about?

DRUMPF
Visions of prophecy!

GUY
You seem to have a lot of vision going on there.

DRUMPF
My vision is filling the entire room ...   1000

HOT DOG MAN
I've got a whole penthouse and two hotels full.

GUY
Now where are you gettin' these visions from?

DRUMPF
Mine are the visions from a high authority!

HOT DOG MAN
Mine are the visions on the authority of being high!

72

GUY *(to* **DRUMPF***)*
What are these visions about?

DRUMPF
About our country, about my success,
About you, about me, about everything, really.
GUY *(to* **HOT DOG MAN***)*
And what are yours about?

HOT DOG MAN
About our country, about grabbing stuff,
About them other people, about avoiding crabs,
About the day-traders whittling away everyone's daily bread,
About you, about me. This guy can bite me!   1010

GUY
Come on now. Lay out your visions for me.
I especially like that one about me flyin'
Like an eagle over the mansion on the hill.

DRUMPF
Hear now, then, and listen to this:
"Mark ye, O Native Son, the Way of the Word,
Which God yawped from yon distant High Mount,
He bids ye to preserve that shaggy dog,
Teller of stories and tweeter against fake news,
Who wags for you and hrumpfs on your behalf,
Who will generate winning or else bring disaster,
Opposed by the many brayings of donkeys. Haters!"   1020

GUY
In the name of the heartland, I don't get it.
Native Sons, dogs and donkeys?

DRUMPF
The watchdog is ME, because I howl on your behalf.
The vision says to protect me, your dog.[53]

HOT DOG MAN
That's not what the vision means.
It says that this dog here
Makes you his bitch, humping your leg.[54]
I can reveal the true vision to you.

GUY
Go 'head then. Let me get a stick first, though,
'case that pit bull vision bites me in the ass!

HOT DOG MAN

"Beware, Native Son, that junk yard dog,   1030
Who, while thou harken to his rascally tweets,
Wags his tail at the pollsters and devours your budgets,
Plying revenues while workers remain wretched.
And he will raid your homes, bitch,
While you're slack-jawed, distracted by media mavens,
Licking clean your plates and prestige."

GUY

I like this high prophecy of yours!

DRUMPF

My good man, listen here and then render your verdict:
"In the holy land made great again shall be born
A lion, fiercely guarding the people,
Flitting away the multitudinous mosquitoes with
His twittery tail. This creature do you
Protect, building a stone wall and a house of covfefe."[55]   1040
Do you understand that?

GUY

Heck no.

DRUMPF

The god is clearly saying that you ought to protect me.
Since, for you I am the best lion there is.

GUY

Are you sure it doesn't say that you are the best AT lyin'?

HOT DOG MAN

The real question is what does it mean
To build a stone wall and a house of "covfefe?"

GUY

Yeah, what is covfefe anyway?

HOT DOG MAN

I think it means if he stonewalls you, you should lock him in the Big
House.

GUY

That prophecy can be fulfilled any minute now ...   1050

DRUMPF

Fake news! Jealous jackdaws twittering away,
But rather love your eagle-spirited defender. Keep him in your heart.
Who has made Athens great again and drained the swamp of Spartans.[56]

74

HOT DOG MAN
Bah. Drumpf only shows courage out of delusion.
Ill-informed Son of Liberty, why do ye think your deeds great?
"A woman may bear a load, if a man piles it onto her.
And she couldn't resist. She's shit out of luck if she resists" Isn't that
your view?

DRUMPF
Believe me. There were polls predicting my primacy! Everyone knew.
Polls predicted me bigly.

GUY
What polls? What's he talking about?

HOT DOG MAN
He's always talking about his pole size. Ignore it.[57]   1060

GUY
I'm just worried about where he'll try and stick his pole!

HOT DOG MAN
The next prophecy is about the troops,
So you should definitely respect it.

GUY
I'm listening. Predict on. The pay.
How are we going to support our boys in uniform?

HOT DOG MAN
"O Son of Liberty, beware the Heffalump, lest he trump you,
Deceitful, dancing crazy like a fox, and terribly-twittered."
You get what that's about?

GUY
Well, I've heard of the Heffalump.

HOT DOG MAN
Not that part. It means you have to protect your freedom from budget   1070
items he's always proposing. It's a commandment to refuse them.

GUY
What's a Heffalump have to do with the troops?

HOT DOG MAN
Because a Heffalump and his military plans are equally crazy ideas.

GUY
What kind of a lump is a Heffalump, then?

HOT DOG MAN
It refers to soldiers heaving their lumps, if you catch my drift.

GUY

So who's going to pay our heavy lumpers?

HOT DOG MAN

I'll find a way—and I'll do it better than anyone ever before!
"But lend me your ears, for a sooth to be said,   1080
Lest Kintyre be mulled in your head."

GUY

What's Kintyre?

HOT DOG MAN

The prophecy means this guy looking for a handout:
"Gimme somethin', mister, so I kin tie one on."

DRUMPF

Wrong! It means everyone can tire of you.
But I've got another prophecy about you:
On winged words you will fly like an eagle
Around the whole earth under your rule.

HOT DOG MAN

I have that, too, but the earth and beyond, too, to the Red Sea
So you'll rule over your harem and lick spotted dick.

DRUMPF

Wait! I have a dream! I dream I see Lady Liberty herself   1090
Flooding the ordinary guy with milk and honey.

HOT DOG MAN

I also have a dream! I dream I see Lady Liberty herself
Arrives from the city with Athens' sacred owl,
And from a gorgeous chalice pouring out
Divine sweetness on you and ghost-pepper sauce on him.

GUY

HOOOOOOOOOOOOOOOOOOOOO-whee!
Now that's some visioning right there!
I am all yours, buddy. You are my personal
Trainer, academic advisor, and gerontologist.

DRUMPF

No, no, not yet, PLEASE.   1100
I'll provide a food subsidy and a stipend for you.

GUY

No more welfare. I've been swamped enough
By you and your deplorables.

76

DRUMPF
But I'll give you so much bread you'll be tired of chewing!

HOT DOG MAN
I'll do better than bread. Soft sesame seed buns for me
Two all-beef patties and the rest. You deserve a break today!

GUY
All right, here's what we're gonna do.
Whichever of you two can do me righter,
That's who gets to represent me.

DRUMPF
Out of my way! I need to go inside first.

HOT DOG MAN
No no, me!   1110
(**DRUMPF** *and* **HOT DOG MAN** *pummel their way inside.*)
(*inspired by "Cabinet Battle #1" from Hamilton*)

CHORUS
Guy, lovely is the People's authority,
When all o' Greek people revere yer Guy's tyranny,
But don't enjoy flatterizing deceptions,
While you're absent in your cogitations!   1120

GUY
But cowboys c'n forget,
My brain could really operate beneath this hair,
If'n you're thinkin' that I am not aware,
Now raisin' ev'ry demagogue in Attica town
So I can smack 'em on down.   1130

CHORUS
So y'all are a-densely deliberate, I see,
Preparing yourself some treats
For your dessert you do got a barbecue deal,
In the twitterverse, expose sinful misdeeds
Till you fatten 'em an' make sacrificed meals.   1140

GUY
My intelligence is a tremendous command,
I'm pretending so criminal klepto cannot understand
I'm always with my wits as they try their stealin',
Yet I never let anything slip past me,
So whatever they've stolen, I get repaid.
I vote to convict 'em when they try to make me prepay!   1150

DRUMPF
Hey! Get the hell out of my way!

HOT DOG MAN
You get out of mine, jerk.

DRUMPF
Hey Guy, check me out. I've been lying here, let me tell you,
For THE longest time—forever and ever wanting to service you.[58]

HOT DOG MAN
And I've been sitting here for THE longest time times ten.
No, times a thousand. No, a million! No, times infinity!

GUY
I feel your pain. Waiting for you two is like an eternal enema.
My bowels have earned an evacuation times infinity!

HOT DOG MAN
You know what to do, right?

GUY
I certainly do ... you just say it first.

HOT DOG MAN
Put me and him at the starting gate
And make it a race to do you right.

GUY
Yes! That's it!   1160
On your marks!

DRUMPF & **HOT DOG MAN**
Ready!
Set!

GUY
Go!

The two jostle each other crashing and bumbling off stage so they can keep coming back with the various props listed below (furniture and picnic baskets).

HOT DOG MAN
Stay outta my lane, mofo!

GUY (*bantering with the audience, since he is alone on stage for a slight second*)
Hmm, I'm going to get super lucky with my lover boys today,
Or maybe I'll just suddenly "get a headache."

DRUMPF (*running back onstage*)
Look here! I brought a comfy chair for you first!

HOT DOG MAN (*hot on his heels, shoving him aside*)
But no table! I brought that even first-ier!

DRUMPF
Look here. I'm bringing you these large soft buns (*as he is bending over the basket, butt wiggling to the audience*)
Freshly kneaded. I've got dough! I'm a doughy fellow!

HOT DOG MAN
And I've got you some nice finger food
Fingered from the snatch—I mean—snatched from the fingers
Of our Lady Liberty

GUY
Lady Liberty must have quite a huge ... finger.   1170

DRUMPF
And I have for you some thick, creamy pea soup.
You'll love it. Freshly pounded out by our master chef.

HOT DOG MAN
Hey Guy, that's some god-given gumbo you got.
She really pours her grace on thee.

GUY
Oh yeah!
From pea to shining pea!

DRUMPF
And she wants YOU! She has offered you a piece of her meat.

HOT DOG MAN
And the First Lady has presented to you some cheesecake
Plus two coconuts and her prize-winning melons.

GUY
That's very kind of her to remember my just desserts!   1180

DRUMPF
The commander-in-chief suggests that you try some freedom fries.
Support the troops! Make Athens Great Again!

HOT DOG MAN
Take these, too.

GUY
Hot crossed buns? Whatta I do with these?

HOT DOG MAN
It's making sure our country takes care of our troops.
They cross themselves and they're always happy to see hot buns!

And here's a drink to fill up your tank, premium ... if you get my drift.

GUY (*Tastes, shudders happily as it kicks in.*)
Nice. That's one high octane drink.

HOT DOG MAN
Quite a kick and plenty of horsepower!

DRUMPF
Excuse me! Excuse me! Have a piece of my pie.   1190

HOT DOG MAN
You're excused. Here's the whole pie!

DRUMPF
You won't be able to top this:
Rare, imported, endangered and protected shark steak.

HOT DOG MAN
D'oh! Where can I get a real shark steak?
Come on, brain, what scheme can you find for me?

DRUMPF
See this? Sucks to be you!

HOT DOG MAN
Not interested. I'm watching foreign couriers
Looking to liquidate illicit assets.

DRUMP
Where? Where?

> HOT DOG MAN *swipes the plate of shark steak.*

HOT DOG MAN
What do you care? Keep the foreigners out, right?
Guy, buddy, look what I got you!

DRUMPF
Hey! That's my private property you took credit for!   1200

HOT DOG MAN
Just the way you take credit for others' government work.

GUY
DUDE! You gotta tell me: how'd you come up with that snatching idea?

HOT DOG MAN
The snatch is the goddess'.
But I did the actual grabbing myself.

DRUMPF
But I'm the one who actually swam in the shark tank![59]

GUY
Get outta here! Ya snooze ya looze.

DRUMPF
Oh no, I'm going to be out-deplorabled! Sad!

HOT DOG MAN
Come on, Guy, just stop now and decide which of us
is the better man for you
and your gut.

GUY
OK, but what alternative fact will convince the audience
That I'm making a sound conclusion?   1210

HOT DOG MAN
I'll tell you: tip-toe over to my cart
And inspect the contents inside.
And then Drumpf's.
Don't worry: you'll make the right choice.

GUY
I'll have a look. So what's in here?

HOT DOG MAN
It's empty, right?
Who's my daddy? I gave you everything I had.

GUY
All right! This is a cart that stands with the People! The People's Cart!

HOT DOG MAN
Now stroll on over here to Drumpf's.
What do you see?

GUY
OMG! It's stuffed with all kinds of awesome shit!
There's a whole feast in here!
He only trickled down to me scraps from the kiddie menu!   1220

HOT DOG MAN
Typical. And he's been scheming against you all along:
He delivers some slurp of economic prosperity
But he gulps the goodies himself.

GUY
You jackass! You just robbed and cheated me!
I made you leader of the free world!

DRUMPF
But I descended to the swamp to make Athens great again.

GUY

Get over here and down on your knees.
I'm stripping you of your office and transferring the powers to him.

HOT DOG MAN

You heard him: down on your knees!
Douchebag.

DRUMPF

Not yet!
I feel the voice of righteousness coursing through me!
Hear the word of the Lord, by what like of man alone
I am to be bested.   1230

HOT DOG MAN

Say my name, bitch—and spell it out loud!

DRUMPF

Not so fast: I want to examine your testimony.
See if you agree with the Word from On High.
First, swear, under oath so help you god,
As a child, what school did you go to?

HOT DOG MAN

Public School District 69 ½:
The real school of hard knocks ground me into meat.

DRUMPF

Huh, what'd you say?
That's what I heard the voice say ...
OK, next:
What did you do in after-school sports?

HOT DOG MAN

When you're stealing a base—look 'em right in the eye and lie.

DRUMPF

Oh Lord, why hast thou forsaken me!   1240
When you grew up, how did you make a living?

HOT DOG MAN

I sold hot dogs and I was sold doggy style. We all gotta pay the rent.[60]

DRUMPF

This is horrible! I am doomed! Sad!
There is but one hope of salvation remaining.
Tell me this now: did you sling your meat
In the business district or downtown?

82

HOT DOG MAN
Downtown. As low down as you can go.

DRUMPF
Horrid!
The word of God fulfilled!
Take this poor damned soul away!
Goodbye and farewell, dear executive power.
Curtain down! Play's over for this actor. Off to the dressing room!   1250
Alas, poor office! I knew it, Horatio, a corner
With infinite desk, of most excellent fancy. I did
Sign on its dotted lines a thousand times, but nevermore …

HOT DOG MAN
(looks and points up with both hands)
The victory is yours!

CHORUS
All hail the wiener winner! Sick of winning yet?
And remember:
I'm the one who made you a man.
And just a quick favor:
Let me be your "right hand" man.

GUY
Now it's time to tell me your real name.

HOT DOG MAN
Frank Street Weiser, cuz I'm the wisest hot-dog dude on the streets.

GUY
Then, Frank Street Weiser, I formally designate you my representative,
And remand the Drumpf here to your custody.   1260

HOT DOG MAN
And Guy, you can be sure that I will faithfully fight for your interests,
And you'll have to say that no one's ever
Been a better ally and friend to the land of the free and home of the
depraved.[61]

CHORUS
(inspired by "Beer for My Horses")
Cuz' beauty is the best thing we can try to find,
We gotta saddle up our rhymes,
We gotta zing up our lines.
When Apollo says it, we'll sing a victory hymn
And we'll comfort all the hungry homeless,   1270
We'll raise up our skyphoi against evil forces,

Singing
"Sangria for my men,
Barley for my horses."
Now,
There ain't nothin' wrong 'bout calling out scum:
'mounts to bein' upright toward good honest folk,
If you think 'bout it right.
Now we know some mighty fine people.
And they got people that they're related to.
And those relations ain't worth cookin' up a cow patty for.   1290
In fact, we would go so far as to refuse cookin' up an otherwise
Perfectly fine cow patty, for no other reason than to deny
These shit eaters what they want!
And they don't stop there!
Some o' these same folks go on lickin' the morning dew offa
Some ladies of ill-repute with their tongues, and not because it's that
time of day,
If you get my meanin'.
Now I believe in sharing a brew with any decent man in my company,
But for these folks, I'm makin' an exception and keepin' my mug to
myself.
It ain't slanderin' for to tongue lash deplorables,
For good folk consider it an honor, if you think about it.
If some ol' boy, the target of these here attacks
Is in the public eye—well, I'd never mention a friend,
But I think everyone knows who we're talking about.
No sense in hiding the truth behind a white hood here.
Y'all know who our target is from the play,
Despite the years separatin' the ancient author from now.
He's a deplorable fella! Actually, he wishes he were deplorable.[62]
He's not only deplorable—I'd have let that go
He's uber-deplorable. He's broken every record for deplorablity
He's stained his tongue with deesgusting pleasures.
You heard what he did with those foreign hoes:
The golden opportunity for golden showers,
Soaking his golden hair on a golden bed.
Cavorting with supremacists and thugs.
Whoever doesn't completely reject all association with
A guy like this, should never share a brew with me.
(back to "Beer for My Horses")
Cuz' justice is the one thing we should always find,
We've hadda saddle up at night,
We've hadda scratch up our minds.

84

Why poor man's table yields to the 1%'s food,
When we could just market our laborer's fruit,
And raise up our skyphoi against evil forces,
Singing
"Sangria for my men,
Barley for my horses."
There's talk about some battleships that got to gossipin' 1300
And one of them old ladies said,
"Hey, girls, ain't you gonna talk about what's happening?
Talk of sending us to totally destroy a country.
The sus-Pence of the idea is shocking!"
The others agreed this was an intolerable disgrace.
One of them, who'd never taken on seamen, said,
"God forbid! I'll never let that man boa'd me!
If I must, I'll grow old here, cobwebs in my portholes.
No! He will not walk my plank, gods no!
That man will never shiver my well-made timbers!" 1310
If that's what the country really wants,
Then, in my opinion, we should anchors aweigh—
Cut loose and sail off into the setting sun without them.
He'll not mock our city by becoming one of our commanders.
He can sail off the deep end, instead, if that's what he wants.
Let him sail back to the Atlantic City from whence he came!

HOT DOG MAN
Let all present observe silence, keep their mouths shut,
refrain from testifying, and keep the courts closed
(no matter how much you all are addicted to courtroom drama),
So that we may make a presentation to you spectators,
For your appreciative commendation.

CHORUS
O shining brilliance of holy Athens, shepherd of her empire,
With what good word do you fill the streets? What's that delicious
odor? 1320

HOT DOG MAN
I've boiled Guy down so much he's right handsome instead of icky.

CHORUS
So where is he now, you marvelous miracle worker?

HOT DOG MAN
He is at home in Athens—land of the free and the home of the brave.

CHORUS
How may we see him? How does he look? What's his new costume?

HOT DOG MAN

He's like he was when he fought alongside the Greatest Generation,
When they were his constant companions.[63] But you'll get to see him.
You can hear the pearly gates opening even now.
Now give it up for the return of Old-School Athens,
Honored with miracles and song, home of the free, the brave, and the
Guy!

CHORUS

O Athens, let your light shine,
may your skies be spacious and your waves of grain be amber!
May you be the envy of the world!
Bestow upon us the sole
ruler of this our land. 1330

HOT DOG MAN

Behold! Restored to the splendor of form from the ages gone by,
Redolent not of mothballs but now he smells like teen spirit!

CHORUS

Hello, ruler of the Greeks! We're delighted to see you!
You've earned the city's respect and truly are of the greatest generation![64]

GUY

Frank Street Weiser, best of best friends, come to me.
You have done a world of good to me by boiling me down.

HOT DOG MAN

Really?
Dude, if you had any idea what you were like before,
And what I've done, you'd call me an intervention god.

GUY

Go on, tell me: what'd you have to do? How bad was I?

HOT DOG MAN

Well first, whenever anybody went up to the Assembly and said, 1340
"I'm on your side, Guy. I alone am your lover boy![65]
I want you, I need you, I ain't never gonna leave you!"
Just at those words, you'd flap and leap around
Like a happy chicken or a horny goat.

GUY

Ouch.

HOT DOG MAN

He'd get your votes for nothing but empty promises.

GUY
What? Really?
They did me that way and I didn't even know?

HOT DOG MAN
Absolutely. Your ears would flail open
Just like an umbrella, then shut tight up again.

GUY
I was such a senile dumbass …

HOT DOG MAN
God yeah.
If two politicians made proposals: 1350
One for defense, one for subsidies,
The subsidies would win out.
Hey, can't you stand up? Are you fainting?

GUY
I'm just so ashamed of my former screw-ups.

HOT DOG MAN
It's not your fault. Don't take it that way.
It's those haters. Come on now.
Try this: if some bombastic political clown says,
"No daily bread for the average joe
Unless you declare this other guy here a criminal!"   1360
What are you gonna do to that talking head?

GUY
I'll throw 'im into a REAL swamp with lobbyists hanging from his neck.

HOT DOG MAN
Now you're talking with some real sense!
Keep going. Let me hear you. Lay some policy on me.

GUY
Well first I'm gonna make sure that all our boys in uniform
Get the treatment they need and pay they deserve when they get home.

HOT DOG MAN
A lotta jar-heads are gonna be happier than pigs in a jar of shit at that.

GUY
And anybody else in the civil service, no special favors.   1370
Everyone does the job assigned to them without interference.

HOT DOG MAN
That'll be a blow to those fortunate sons!

GUY
And none o' those smoothy slimeballs anymore!

HOT DOG MAN
Out of business for Effete and Douche, Hedge Fund Ltd!

GUY
No, I meant those perfumed pipsqueaks
Who sit around mouthbreathing nonsense.
"That guy's brilliant! Can you believe he got away with it?
His argument's unbreakable, his logic unstoppable.
His twittering's brutal, his memes are dope.
Ringing endorsements, best mass beat-downs."   1380

HOT DOG MAN
So, the babblers get the thumbs down and the middle finger up?

GUY
Nah, I'll knock em out o' their knickers back to nature.

HOT DOG MAN
For that good service, then, have this here recliner
And a young man to push it into position for you.
And if you like, you can push him into position on the recliner, too.[66]

GUY
Well, bless my soul, now I really do feel old-school!

HOT DOG MAN
When I hand over the long-term peace accords for you to ratify,
Then you can really say that. Thirty-year peace accords, come on out!

(Attractive young "ACCORDS" come out and act friendly with GUY.)

GUY
Glory, glory, glory! Those are some pretty peaces! By god,   1390
What, are they seventeen years each? Let's double our pleasure!
How'd you get 'em, anyway?

HOT DOG MAN
Actually,
Drumpf was hiding them away inside, so you couldn't have them.
So now I bestow them upon you, to go forth to plow the fields
And prosper.

GUY
Oooh, that Drumpf!
Tell me what you're gonna do with him for all he did?

HOT DOG MAN

Not much really. He'll take my old job,
Stuffing sausages when the city gates open up,
Mixing dog and donkey meat into his business,
Getting drunk, screaming at the cheap whores,   1400
Slurping drips from the public bathrooms.

GUY

You sure figured out what he deserves:
Shoutstorms with whores and shit cleaners: Reality Tragedy!
As a reward, let me offer you dinner downtown,
In the seat that (*indicating* **DRUMPF**) tumor of a turd used to sit on.
Follow me and put on this sharp dinner suit.
And someone take the trash (*again indicating* **DRUMPF**) out to his new job,
So all the foreigners he harassed can see where he belongs!

NOTES

1 "Drumpf" in this translation of the play was named "Paphlagon" in the original. That name referred to the character's supposed Paphlagonian, i.e., non-Athenian, ancestry. That name is a way of marking the illegitimacy of the character for the role of significance in Athens that he holds; people who are not born of two Athenian citizens are not eligible for citizenship and its benefits, including participation in affairs of government. See introduction, xxviii, for more explanation.

2 The archaic formality of the language reflects Nicias' effort to sound refined in quoting line 345 from the Athenian tragedy *Hippolytus*, written and produced by Euripides in 428 BCE. Phaedra addresses the Nurse in the line.

3 *Demos*, in Greek, can mean "the people," as in the populace as a whole, or something closer to "the masses," a derogatory term for the non-elite majority of the citizen body. "[O]f Main Street" is used here in place of "of the Pnyx," the place where the Athenian assembly, which every Athenian citizen was eligible to attend, met. The name of this character and his close connection to life on the ground in Athens reflects the class of people that Cleon, the person who inspired Drumpf, successfully sought to win over in Athenian life outside of the play to further his political ambitions. See introduction, xxvii-xxviii, for more explanation.

4 The family of Cleon, the most powerful politician in Athens at the time, and who was the model for Paphlagon/Drumpf, made its fortune running a leather goods factory. Cleon himself was regularly conflated with the workers (most of them enslaved) who worked in his family's factory.

5 Demosthenes and Cleon led a successful assault in 425 against a Spartan force trapped on the island of Sphacteria, off the west coast of Greece; see the introduction for more information about that situation. Though Thucydides' *History of the Peloponnesian War* treats Cleon as having been effective in his planning and leadership of the attack, Demosthenes laid the groundwork for it by trapping the Spartans on the island at the Battle of Pylos. He also may have been more critical than Cleon in the strategizing and implementation of the attack.

6 This appears to be a reference to Eucrates of Melite, who may be the same Eucrates who was a general in 432/1 in Macedonia.

7 This is Lysicles, who lived with Aspasia, the powerful general Pericles' wife, after Pericles died in 429. Lysicles himself died in 428.

8 The choice of this line of work for Drumpf's fated successor appears to be fanciful, rather than a reference to anyone particular in Athenian life.

9 This is a reference to a privileged position that Cleon (represented by

90

Drumpf) held. One tangible reward that he received for pushing for and taking part in the assault on Sphacteria was the opportunity to eat meals each day in the Prytaneum, the building designated for the executives (*prytaneis*) of each year's council (*boule*). See introduction, xxi–xxiii, for more about this situation. This building was a site of civic business, but also of dining, not just for the *prytaneis*, but also distinguished foreign visitors and other notable Athenians, such as Athens' Olympic champions and those who had been granted honors for contributions to Athens' wellbeing.

10   In Greek, this line is, literally, "because you are working-class (*poneros*), out of the marketplace (*ex agoras*), and bold." To be "out of the marketplace" means having spent significant amounts of time amidst the crush of people buying and selling goods and services, and otherwise hanging around a place where there were lots of people of rather humble social status; the equivalent of it in American life would be something like "from the streets."

11   The word here is, again, a form of *poneros*, which means, effectively, "working class."

12   The word translated as "political leadership" is *demagogia*; this is the first time that a use of the word from which "demagogy" and "demagogue" derive appears in extant literature.

13   The Greek word for "popular leadership" here is *demagogika*, or "demagogic things." This is the earliest attestation of this word anywhere.

14   The Greek word translated as "low class" is *agoraios*, which has, as one of its meanings, "fitting in in the marketplace." The significance of the *agora* and those who spend time there is explained in n. 10, and the agora itself is mentioned multiple times in the rest of the play.

15   Actors in the classical Greek theatre wore wooden or linen masks during performances; among other things, this allowed the three actors provided to each playwright/director to play multiple roles without confusion as to which one each was playing in a given scene. See introduction, xxiv, for more information about this. For the original performance, mask-makers were apparently unwilling to risk the consequences that could come from taking a direct role in mocking the most powerful figure in Athens.

16   The Greek word here is *panourgos*, "all-worker," an expression for a thief.

17   This is a reference to the honor that Cleon received that allowed him to eat daily lunches at the Prytaneum, see n. 9.

18   The Greek is *poneros*, "working class." See nn. 10 and 11 for previous uses of this term.

19   In Greek, this translates directly as "nail the generals at Pylos," a reference to Cleon's receiving credit for the successful invasion of Sphacteria, off the

coast of Pylos.

[20] Hot Dog Man consistently takes on a role of sexual agent, or proud recipient of penetration as part of a previous job. Portrayals of Drumpf's close interactions are typically either sexually passive or, more commonly, conspicuously expressing relations of friendship with Demos, rather than sexual desire. See introduction, xxvi-xxvii, for more discussion of this.

[21] The Greek refers to a festival of *Zeus Agoraios*, "Zeus of the Marketplace," another notice of the significance to political success of spending time with the common Athenians where they gather in large numbers.

[22] The Greek is *pamponere*, "all-working-class."

[23] Here is more sexual explicitness from Hot Dog Man.

[24] There are lots of references in Old Comedy to politicians taking passive roles in homosexual relationships, which was out of step with adult men's expected sexual behavior. See introduction, xxvi-xxvii, for standard practices in Athenian pederasty.

[25] Another reference to explicit sexuality concerning Hot Dog Man.

[26] The following speech/song by the Chorus is the play's *parabasis*, the "coming forward" of the chorus. This was a typical feature of Athenian Old Comedies, in which choruses would speak directly to the audience about matters of contemporaneous politics and/or arts. All choral interludes were sung and danced to the accompaniment of an *aulos*, a two-piped flute. See introduction, xxiv-xxvi, for more information about structures of Athenian comedies.

[27] In Greek, "the spirit of the streets" is *Zeus Agoraios*, "Zeus of the Marketplace." (See also line 410, with n. 21.)

[28] In the original, the Chorus talks about how difficult it is to be both writer and director of these publicly-performed comedies, and how ever-changing public tastes led to comic playwrights who were celebrated at one time being mocked not long thereafter.

[29] This is a complicated passage in the Greek. It literally says, "I LIKE you, and I want to be your lover." The word for "like" can often cross over into meaning "love," in a romantic sense, but it is not, typically, the expression used by a pursuing partner. The use of "like" with "lover" nods to the complexity of Drumpf's position relative to Demos—Aristophanes wants to use the "lovers" imagery to make the connection between Drumpf and Demos humorous, but recognizes that Drumpf's/Cleon's method of connection with supporters was mainly through friendship. See introduction for more about lines between pederasty and friendship and Cleon's apparent methods of outreach to his supporters.

30   Hot Dog Man, in turn, refers to himself as a "competing lover," but uses an expression of affection that is much more typical for a desirous lover: *erao*, "I desire."

31   He is referring to the Athenian assembly, which every male adult citizen was eligible to attend.

32   Drumpf speaks again not as a lover does, but as a friend does, in terms of service to Demos.

33   Hot Dog Man here initially follows Drumpf's lead, using *phileo* and *stergo*, for "love" and "adore," both of which express friendly affection, but then turns to sexuality, with the phallic "wiener sack" and wish to be dragged "by the balls."

34   Once again, the word Drumpf uses is *phileo*, "I like," or "I love," primarily in the context of friends and family members.

35   In the Greek, Drumpf refers to the steps that he took as a member of the randomly-chosen *boule* (council) to collect taxes for the benefit of the Athenian people.

36   Hot Dog Man uses *phileo* to claim that Drumpf does NOT like Demos.

37   In the Greek, Hot Dog Man brings up the battles of Marathon (490 BCE) and Salamis (480 BCE), which happened 66 and 56 years, respectively, before the first performance of this play, to tie Demos back to glorious moments in Athenian history in which almost no one in the audience would have taken part.

38   In the Greek, Demos asks if Hot Dog Man is connected to Harmodius, who, along with his boyfriend Aristogeiton, assassinated Hipparchus, the brother of the tyrant Hippias, in 514. That celebrated murder set Athens on a course to establishing the first form of its democracy in 509. Cleon's wife seems to have had a family connection to Harmodius, and Cleon may have tried to benefit from that tie. Demos seems to suggest that anyone (in this case, Hot Dog Man) who shows such democratic leanings must have such a connection.

39   The Greek includes *philodemos*, "liking the people."

40   Again, the word for "love" in the Greek is *phileo*.

41   *Phileo* again.

42   The Greek here is specifically *panourgeis*, "crime-committing."

43   Again, the word for "love" in the Greek is *phileo*.

44   This line makes explicit what appears to be one of Cleon's pitches to the

Athenian people, which Drumpf reflects: he was their friend, with all of the benefits that accompany that relationship.

45   Again, the word for "love" in the Greek is *phileo*. In the original text, the offer that Hot Dog Man claims that Drumpf had been withholding was of replacement soles for worn-out leather shoes; Cleon's family business was leather goods, so that would be the sort of product closely associated with him. On a different level, though, the discussion of doing favors for Guy is another area that blurs relationships of pederasty and friendship. Lovers in pursuit of boyfriends had to be careful in offering gifts to the boys (or in this case, men) that they were pursuing, for fear of making the pursued feel like prostitutes. Among friends, though, favors were a way of showing one's investment in a relationship; the expectation is that they would be reciprocated appropriately.

46   In the original text, it was a long-sleeved tunic that Hot Dog Man gave to Guy. Once again, valuable gifts are problematic for a lover on the make to give to a boyfriend; they can imply that the boyfriend does not have the resources to provide for himself. Among friends, though, such gifts are understood as being reciprocated in some other way.

47   Though details of this situation are lost, Cleon had apparently arranged for low prices on silphium, a now-extinct plant in the family of fennel and celery, which had a side effect of producing gas in its consumers.

48   In the original text, the offer was of a wage, paid by the state, that was not connected to work—i.e., a dole, or universal basic income. While Cleon himself is not on record as having proposed such a thing, one of the demagogues who followed in his wake, Cleophon, successfully passed a measure for it later in the fifth century BCE. It is thus likely that *someone* was talking about such a practice at the time of this play.

49   Unsurprisingly, the Greek term for the affection expressed here is *phileo*.

50   In the original text, the discussion is of Paphlagon returning Guy's ring; Guy discovers that Drumpf is wearing someone else's ring instead, indicating that he has not been faithfully committed to Guy.

51   In the Greek, there is a description here of the image on the ring that Paphlagon is wearing—it is of a seagull (i.e., a big-mouthed creature, to which Cleon is also compared in Aristophanes' *Clouds*) squawking to a crowd, the sort of thing that helped Cleon reach his current level of prominence.

52   The wineskin images here refer, unsurprisingly, to sexual activity. The different ways they are used, though, are revelatory. Drumpf implies that Hot Dog Man will penetrate Guy's anus, while Hot Dog Man suggests that Guy's sexual organ would be in action more if he were to align himself with Drumpf. The difference seems to hearken back to the distinction between how each demagogue views Guy: Hot Dog Man sees him more as an object of

desire, while to Drumpf, he is more a friend; this likely reflects Cleon's own language and actions toward common Athenians.

53 A dog is much like a friend—it provides beneficial service for its human family in exchange for beneficial services to it (i.e., a home, food, and love). The fact that Cleon is referred to as a watchdog in two other plays of Aristophanes as well (*Wasps* and *Peace*) suggests that he likely described himself as such to the Athenian people.

54 In the original text, the dog's offense is sneaking bites of gruel from its masters.

55 In the original, "covfefe" is "iron towers."

56 This refers to Cleon's success at the Battle of Sphacteria.

57 In the Greek, there is a play on the words Pylos (where the Athenian force was staged before attacking Sphacteria) and *puelos*, "a tub."

58 The Greek for what Drumpf offers is *euergetein*, "to do a good deed."

59 In the original, the discussion was over who deserved credit for the victory at Sphacteria. Some Athenians treated Cleon as having just benefited from Demosthenes' excellence as a general in planning and carrying out the invasion, while Drumpf's retort is that it was he (Cleon) who took the initiative to press for the attack at that time, when others thought that any attack on the Spartans on land was unjustifiably dangerous.

60 Hot Dog Man implies that he acted as a prostitute in his youth, one more way in which his sexuality is notably more explicit than Drumpf's.

61 "Home of the depraved" is the translation for the Greek *Kekhenaion*, "Gaping-mouthed-enians," apparently referring to Athenians as gaping-mouthed fools, as fellators, or both.

62 In the Greek text, the Chorus attacks several contemporaneous Athenians, the actions of whom are almost entirely lost to us.

63 In the original version, the people with whom Guy is associated are Aristides and Miltiades, prominent figures in Athens' resistance to the Persian Empire's attack in the early fifth century BCE.

64 In the original, this was a reference to the Battle of Marathon; see n. 37, for explanation.

65 In the Greek, this is an exact quote of what Drumpf says to Guy at line 732.

66 Hot Dog Man seizes upon another opportunity to make a sexual reference.

Made in the USA
Middletown, DE
09 October 2022